THE WHITE SLAVE TRADE AND THE IMMIGRANTS:

A CHAPTER IN AMERICAN SOCIAL HISTORY

By

FRANCESCO CORDASCO

Montclair State College

Former Visiting Professor, City University of New York

with

THOMAS MONROE PITKIN

Former Chief Historian, United States National Park Service

Foreword by

David N. Alloway, Montclair State College

Blaine Ethridge - Books   13977 Penrod Street   Detroit, Michigan 48223   U.S.A.

The second half of this book is a reproduction
of a Senate document entitled, *Importation
and Harboring of Women for Immoral Purposes.*
Only the pagination has been changed.

Manufactured in the United States of America.

*PLEASE WRITE FOR A FREE, ANNOTATED CATALOG
OF BOOKS ON ETHNICITY AND LATIN AMERICAN
SUBJECTS*

Library of Congress Cataloging in Publication Data

Cordasco, Francesco, 1920-
    The white slave trade and the immigrants.

    "A reproduction of a Senate document entitled,
Importation and harboring of women for immoral
purposes": p.
    Bibliography: p.
    Includes index.
    1. Prostitution--United States. 2. United States—
Emigration and immigration. I. Pitkin, Thomas M.
II. United States. Immigration Commission. Impor-
ting women for immoral purposes. 1981. III. Title.
HQ144.C67   306.7'4'0973   81-1303
ISBN 0-87917-077-8   AACR2

IN MEMORY OF

LAWRENCE M. COHEN

OBIIT JANUARY 20, 1980

WHO LOVED THE IMMIGRANT COMMUNITIES

This importation of women for immoral purposes
has brought into the country evils even worse than those
of prostitution. In many instances the professionals who
come here have been practically driven from their lives
of shame in Europe on account of their loathsome diseases;
the conditions of vice obtaining there have even lowered
the standard of degradation of prostitution formerly customary here. Unnatural practices are brought largely from
continental Europe, and the ease and apparent certainty of
profit have led thousands of our younger men, usually those
of foreign birth or the immediate sons of foreigners, to abandon the useful arts of life to undertake the most accursed
business ever devised by man. This traffic has intensified
all the evils of prostitution which, through the infection of
innocent wives and children by dissipated husbands and
through the mental anguish and moral indignation aroused
by marital unfaithfulness, has done more to ruin homes
than any other single cause.

... The Immigration Commission (1911)

TABLE OF CONTENTS

FOREWORD

There is little question that American scholars have chosen to neglect important phenomena in the social history of the United States: this neglect may be ascribed to a number of complex and interrelated causes. Clearly, the subject which Professor Cordasco and Dr. Pitkin explore in this significant volume would not have been eagerly addressed by social historians in the early decades of this century; the harrowing chronicles of prostitution and the white slave trade would not have appealed to contemporary historians as subjects to be investigated without reference to a larger framework of social inquiry. If we encounter any notices of prostitution and the white slave trade, the encounter is enjoined in the explorations of progressivism and social policy related to the amelioration of social ills. The inquiry into the sordid history of the enslavement of girls in prostitution is always subordinated to the multidimensional portraits of a restive America which is forging its destiny and whose engines are fueled by the multiethnic and racial constituencies which form its disparate populations.

It was not unanticipated that Francesco Cordasco and Thomas Monroe Pitkin would have chosen to have illuminated that dark and forbidding chapter which is the subject of this volume. They have masterfully achieved their objectives. They have clearly shown that the white slave trade was an integral part of that dynamic, evolving America in the period of the great migrations; and they have clearly acquitted the impoverished immigrant masses of that culpability with which they were charged. The white slave trade was, if anything, an indigenous enterprise; the immigrants and their women were only peripherally related to the criminal activity. The narrative of this volume is a kaleidoscope of that cauldron which was American society, and in which one of the dynamic ingredients was criminal endeavor. It is high drama. And it cannot be rejected, or denied its place in American social history. Professor Cordasco and Dr. Pitkin are to be commended for their efforts. This volume will find its audience in American classrooms concerned with the delineation of urban history, the new ethnic studies, the heightened interest in the history of immigration, and in the obsessive fascination with crime.

David N. Alloway
Professor of Sociology
Montclair State College

i

INTRODUCTION

In its encyclopedic study of immigration, the Immigration Commission, convened by the United States Congress in 1907 (and whose *Reports* constituted 41 volumes)[1] did not neglect the white slave trade and the immigrants. In its report on "Importation and Harboring of Women for Immoral Purposes," the Commission observed:

> The importion and harboring of alien women and girls for immoral purposes and the practice of prostitution by them—the so-called "white slave traffic"—is the most pitiful and the most revolting phase of the immigration question. It is in violation of the immigration law and of the agreement of 1904 between the United States and other powers for the repression of the trade in white women. This business had assumed such large proportions and was exerting so evil an influence upon our country that the Immigration Commission felt compelled to make it the subject of a thorough investigation. Since the subject is especially liable to sensational expooitation, the Commission's report is primarily a statement of undeniable facts calculated to form a basis of reasonable legislative and administrative action to lessen its evils.[2]

There is little question that prostitution was a vexing problem to the immigration authorities who administered the offices through which millions of immigrants entered the New World. The Commission, of course, was restrictionist in its views, and prostitution was seen as a peculiarly European accomodation against which the United States had to protect itself:

> Owing to the difference between the European and American views regarding prostitution, cooperation for the suppression of the white-slave traffic can be expected from most of the European nations only along certain lines. Most European countries are rigid in their regulations regarding the procuring for purposes of prostitution of minor girls or of any women by means of fraud and deceit. Women who are of age, however, and who enter the business of their own accord are not interfered with. From continental countries where these conditions exist practically no cooperation could be expected to prevent the sailing of professional prostitutes to the United States. They probably would cooperate to prevent the seduction of minors or the fraudulent or forcible exportation of their women. In the main, however, the United States Government must rely upon its own officials for the prevention of this traffic. (Report, vol. 37, p. 89.)

However xenophobic the view (although there is ample documentation available to illustrate the continuing concern of emigrating nations),[3] the Commission's report on the white slave trade proved "liable to sensational exploitation."

We have endeavoured in the following pages to recreate the historical contexts (largely from contemporary sources) in which the white slave trade existed in the period of the great migrations. We have chosen New York City as our focal point of enquiry not only because it was the major port of immigrant entry, but also because this city provides the most complete extant record of the phenomenon and a multiplicity of responses, official and public: and New York City affords a prototypic model for other cities in the United States and Canada. We have included as a source document the complete text of the Immigration Commission's report on the "Importation and Harboring of Women for Immoral Purposes," a harrowing document, presented to the Congress on December 10, 1909, and following which "steps were immediately taken to amend the immigration law of 1907 to more effectively prevent the importation of women and girls for immoral purposes, and their control by importers or others after admission to the United States."

Our indebtedness is acknowledged to the professional staffs of the New York Public Library, the New York Historical Society, and the New York City Municipal Archives and Records: invariably courteous and helpful, they share in whatever praise this book receives; errors and faults are, of course, ours alone.

F. C.
T. M. P.

---

[1] United States Immigration Commission. *Report of the Immigration Commission.* 41 vols. 61st. Congress. 2nd and 3rd. Sessions. 1911.

[2] *Ibid.,* Vol. 37, p. 57.

[3] The Italian authorities were constantly alert to the problem, as attested by the many references found in the *Bollettino dell'Emigrazione* which recorded the migrations of Italians to all parts of the world. See Francesco Cordasco, *Italian Mass Emigration: The Exodus of a Latin People: A Bibliographical Guide to the Bollettino dell'Emigrazione, 1902-1927.* (Totowa, N.J.: Rowman and Littlefield, 1980).

A NOTE ON IMMIGRATION LITERATURE

An unusually rich literature exists on the social phenomenon of immigration, both in countries of emigration and in immigrant-receiving countries. In the United States, as the result of a new and vigorous ethnic consciousness, immigrant life in America has received a commanding and sustained attention. Academicians in all disciplines have begun to re-examine the fortunes of the diverse groups who peopled America, and given the more sophisticated insights of the new ethnicity, a new social history of America is being written.

Pre-1956 material is available in Francesco Cordasco, ed., *A Bibliography of American Immigration History: The George Washington University Project Studies* (New York: Augustus M. Kelley, 1978): and this may be supplemented by consulting John D. Buenker and Nicholas C. Burckel, eds., *Immigration and Ethnicity: A Guide to Information Sources* (Detroit: Gale Research Company, 1977). Additional references include Josef J. Barton, *Brief Ethnic Bibliography: An Annotated Guide to the Ethnic Experience in the United States* (Cambridge: Langdon Associates, 1976); Francesco Cordasco, *Immigrant Children in American Schools: A Classified and Annotated Bibliography With Selected Source Documents* (Fairfield, N. J.: Augustus M. Kelley, 1976); and Oscar Handlin, *et al,* advisory editors, *The American Immigration Collection,* Series I, 41 vols., Series II, 33 vols. (New York: Arno Press, 1969-1970), a massive reprint program of basic materials on the history of American immigration. An invaluable resource is Stephan Thernstrom, ed., *Harvard Encyclopedia of American Ethnic Groups* (Cambridge: Harvard University Press, 1980). In a class by itself is Robert H. Bremner, *From the Depths: The Discovery of Poverty in the United States* (New York: New York University Press, 1956). A valuable, and in some ways, unique source is Babette F. Inglehart and Anthony R. Mangione, *The Image of Pluralism in American Literature: An Annotated Bibliography on the American Experience of European Ethnic Groups* (New York: American Jewish Committee, 1974).

A mammoth resource is the United States Immigration Commission, *Report of the Immigration Commission,* 41 volumes. (61st Congress, 2nd and 3rd Sessions). Washington: United States Government Printing Office, 1911. Contents: Abstracts, vols. 1-2. Statistical review of immigration; emigration conditions in Europe; dictionary of races and peoples; immigrants in industries; immigrants in cities; occupations of immigrants; fecundity of immigrant women; children of immigrants in schools; immigrants as charity seekers; immigration and crime; steerage conditions; bodily form of descendants of immigrants; federal immigration legislation; state immigration and alien laws; other countries; statements and recommendations. *The Index of Reports of the Immigration Commission* (S. Doc. No. 785, 61st Congress, 3rd Session) was never published. The *Report* was restrictionist in its basic recommendations, and the chairman of the Commission was Senator William P. Dillingham (Massachusetts). The *Report* is summarized in Jeremiah W. Jenks and W. Jett Lauck, *The Immigration Problem: A Study of Immigration Conditions and Needs* (New York: Funk & Wagnals, 1912; 6th ed., 1926). Isaac A. Hourwich, *Immigration and Labor: The Economic Aspects of European Immigration to the United States* (New York: G. P. Putnam Sons, 1912; 2nd ed., 1922), subsidized by the American Jewish Committee, was a statistical attack on the Commission's *Report.*

For a number of complex reasons, American academicians have only rarely chosen to explore the dark side of the immigration phenomenon, the endemic pathology and human disruption which are inherently part of the wrenching of peoples (for whatever reasons) from indigenous countries. Michael M. Passi has perceptively advanced the thesis that ethnic studies in America have been "ironic" in that they have ignored the persistence of ethnic consciousness in American society and instead have sought to demonstrate the process by which ethnic communities have been, or are being, absorbed into an homogenous American culture. (Michael M. Passi, "Mandarins and Immigrants: The Irony of Ethnic Studies in America Since Turner," Ph. D. dissertation, University of Minnesota, 1972). A review of American doctoral literature largely confirms Passi's assessment. In this connection, see Francesco Cordasco and David N. Alloway, *American Ethnic Groups, the European Heritage: A Bibliography of Doctoral Dissertations Completed At American Universities* (Metuchen, N. J.: Scarecrow Press, 1981).

THE WHITE SLAVE TRADE AND THE IMMIGRANTS

I

The New York afternoon papers on November 21, 1902, carried the story of large-scale vice raids in Philadelphia that had revealed the existence of an international ring trafficking in young girls. It was said that the ring had its headquarters in Germany, with branches in Philadelphia and New York, and that its business was to supply girls for disorderly houses in those two cities, in Baltimore, Chicago, and elsewhere. According to reports, the raids had been made at the instance of the German consul in Philadelphia on advice from his ambassador in Washington. Most of the girls picked up in the raids were said to be Jewish, and Rabbi Joseph Krauskopf of the Keneseth Israel Synagogue, who had taken part in the preliminary investigation, was interviewing them. Representatives of the Protestant Episcopal Church and of the Baron de Hirsch colony in Woodbine, New Jersey, were assisting him. It quickly developed that there were French, Italian, and other girls among those picked up and taken to City Hall for examination and trial. The girls were recruited over much of Europe under a variety of false promises, it was reported, shipped through the Port of New York, and sold into absolute slavery.[1]

The *Evening Post,* on receiving the story from Philadelphia, at once interviewed William Williams, the new Commissioner of Immigration at Ellis Island, who had for the past six months been cleaning up a mess of corruption and inefficiency there. Williams knew of no organized traffic in girls, he said, but his staff was on the alert for such cases and every once in a while it found that a girl or young woman had been brought over for immoral purposes. Most of these were brought in as second cabin passengers, who were examined on board the ship and not taken to Ellis Island unless there seemed cause for careful inquiry. It was a delicate matter to handle, he pointed out. If an inspector brought a woman to the island on suspicion that she was an assisted immigrant for immoral purposes, and on investigation it was found that she was all right, there would be a great complaint from the press. He was formulating new rules to make the examination of second cabin passengers more rigid, he said, but as to this particular charge he didn't see that he could do much "unless some one on the other side will inform me when a collection of women are being sent over on some particular ship."[2]

Post reporters also interviewed Inspector Brooks of the Police Department, then recently put in charge of the vice district in mid-Manhattan known as the Tenderloin. Under the reform Fusion administration of Seth Low, elected mayor of New York City the year before, police in plain clothes were making frequent arrests for soliciting in such notorious places as the Haymarket on Sixth Avenue, the Alhambra in 28th Street, and the Savoy, the Cairo, and the Bohemia in 29th Street. They had forced many of the more vicious resorts to close, Brooks said. He was confident that there was no "New York end" to the syndicate alleged to be at work in Philadelphia. Such an operation would be unprofitable. He did admit isolated cases where women and girls were brought in for illicit purposes, but in most such cases, he believed, "the victims are taken directly to other cities." What happened in other cities, obviously, was no concern of the inspector.

District Attorney William Travers Jerome had been elected in the same reform campaign of 1901. He told the *Post* that while the campaign was on and the Tammany Democratic machine still in power, rumors had reached the Committee of Fifteen, organized to investigate vice and gambling in the city, "that girls were systematically brought here for immoral purposes from foreign countries." The Committee, Jerome said, had gone through the city "with a fine tooth comb," but had failed to find any such wholesale iniquity. There might be isolated instances, but he was sure that "no organized band was at work in this city."[3]

The story was developed further the next day. The man suspected by the Philadelphia police of being the head of the ring there had evaded arrest, but three men arrested in the raid were said to be agents. These men "bore Jewish names," *The American Hebrew* noted sadly. Immigration officials in Philadelphia were looking into the matter further, it was said. Officials in New York disclaimed any knowledge of such a conspiracy. The German consul general said he had no official information on the matter, and Commissioner Williams had no communication about it from German officials or from his own superiors in Washington. He knew in a general way that women were brought to this country, but had no definite knowledge of such a traffic as that described in dispatches from Philadelphia. If there was a European syndicate at work, the way to break it up would be to station detectives on the other side. "We can deport a woman who comes for a wrong purpose, but not the person who brings her here," he noted. There was a Federal law making such importation a felony, but it was a very difficult matter to handle. District Attorney Jerome repeated his story that the Committee of Fifteen had looked in vain for an international vice ring at work in the city. It had spent several thousand dollars in trying to unearth a procurers' syndicate such as described in the stories from Philadelphia, he said, "but found no trace of one."[4]

There had been a Federal law on the statute books since 1875 prohibiting the importation of women for purposes of prostitution, and providing penalties for such importation. The law, which also excluded alien convicts and Chinese coolies under contract, was the first Federal legislation restricting immigration. It was designed primarily to curb the Chinese traffic in contract laborers and in women to serve their needs. Most of the cases that had since come up had been on the Pacific Coast and involved Orientals. The first general immigration law was passed in 1882. Another law, passed in 1885, had excluded contract labor in general, and an act of 1891, which established full federal control of immigration, had added other categories of excludable aliens. None of these later laws had mentioned prostitutes or procurers. The international traffic in women, about which there had been a growing agitation in Europe, had not become a matter of concern to Congress.

The rules of the Bureau of Immigration since 1893, under the administrative law passed early in that year, had called for special attention to women coming alone, and matrons had been appointed at Ellis Island to question them. Prostitutes, as such, were not excludable. It had to be determined, under the law of 1875, that they were being imported for immoral purposes. This was rather difficult. Imported prostitutes could also be deported, like other illegal entrants, within one year after their arrival, and occasionally a few such were picked up and sent out of the country after the Commissioner-General of Immigration had issued a circular calling attention to this provision in 1897. But compared to the exclusion and deportation of contract laborers, the diseased, and potential or actual public charges, this was a very incidental activity of the Bureau. A new immigration bill, in whose articulation Commissioner Williams had a hand, was beginning to take form in 1902. It contained specific provisions for the exclusion of prostitutes as such and also for the exclusion of procurers, but it was regarded as merely completing the purpose of the law of 1875, "which makes the importation of such aliens a felony, but omits to provide for rejection at ports of the United States." The subject brought no discussion in Congress and there was no alarm expressed over any systematic traffic in women as the bill moved on to become a law in the following year.[5]

The Philadelphia story was soon dropped by the New York metropolitan papers, but it had roused the increasingly formidable Women's Christian Temperance Union. Under the leadership of Frances Willard, the W.C.T.U. had greatly expanded its original crusade against the demon rum. At its annual convention in 1885, shortly after the *Pall Mall Gazette* had revealed in a series of sensational articles the existence of a thriving traffic in young girls in London and on the Continent, the Union had set up a "White Cross" department, or department of social purity. Miss Willard encountered considerable opposition, the subject being pretty much taboo in polite circles. Nevertheless, she persevered and led the organization in petitioning legislatures for state laws raising the age of consent, for industrial homes for convicted prostitutes and other female offenders, and in general in trying to break down the traditional double standard of conduct in sexual matters. After Miss Willard's death, the W.C.T.U. petitioned Secretary of the Treasury Leslie M. Shaw and President Theodore Roosevelt, to persuade them to appoint women immigrant inspectors. These were to be stationed at Ellis Island, and were to board the incoming liners to inspect the female passengers coming in the first and second cabins.[6]

Various objections to this step were advanced, among them the necessity of setting up a civil service list of eligibles. But Mrs. Margaret D. Ellis, superintendent of legislation for the W.C.T.U. in 1903, circumvented this obstacle by persuading President Roosevelt to suspend the regulations of the Civil Service Commission and allow five young women to be appointed temporarily as immigrant inspectors at the Port of New York. The need was urgent, she felt, and there was no present means of examining cabin passengers along "moral lines." Mrs. Ellis did not believe that a civil service examination would reveal the special qualifications needed, and had already selected five young women engaged in settlement work in New York City. She had also designed a special uniform for them, with bloomers and long skirts. The women inspectors, it was understood, would confine their examinations to girls arriving as first or second cabin passengers whom they might think to have been enticed here by the so-called "Vice Syndicate." Cabin passage, it was understood from the revelations in Philadelphia, was used "to escape the rigorous examination to which the steerage passengers are subjected."

Commissioner Williams, who was soon swamped with applicants for the positions, was highly skeptical of the whole procedure. He insisted that one of the appointees should be an experienced matron from Ellis Island, and rejected two of Mrs. Ellis' list, choosing other applicants. His male boarding inspectors also showed masculine resentment, and openly doubted the ability of young ladies to cope with the job. A veteran boarding officer predicted that they would not last long. They would be terrified by the climb up the ladder of a moving steamer and, once on board, would be disgusted by the sights they would witness.[7]

The inspection of incoming ships for epidemic diseases was then still under New York State administration. Federal immigration officers had no jurisdiction until the ships left their berths at Quarantine and started up the bay. Newspaper reporters and photographers turned out in numbers to watch the appointees climb the swaying ladders up the sides of the moving ships when they first went into action. Sure enough, trouble developed almost at once. On one of the first liners that they boarded off Staten Island, a woman traveling alone in first cabin showed them an address on the West Coast that they believed to be fictitious. Actually, she was going to meet her husband, a merchant sea captain, whose ship was then in port there. She became indignant and then hysterical at the highly personal questions they asked her, and lodged a complaint. The project got off to a very bad start.

While it was later admitted that the women inspectors had detained and sent to Ellis Island a number of young and unprotected girls, they had found "no indication of organized illicit traffic," Williams declared. At the end of 30 days he sent to Commissioner General Frank P. Sargent in Washington a report declaring the experiment a failure. The women were not adding much to the inspection services; they could not detect real prostitutes, and found few girls in cabin class needing help, he said. The chief of the Boarding Division said that second cabin female passengers readily submitted to general inspection by the male inspectors, but resented being singled out for special investigation by female inspectors.[8]

Williams and his staff, who would today no doubt be denounced as male chauvinists, looked for the failure of the experiment and found it. The Commissioner General relayed Williams' negative report to the secretary and he, in turn, notified the Civil Service Commission that no eligible lists would be needed for permanent appointments. Resolutions protesting the removal of the women inspectors were presented to the President by the American Institute of Social Service, but they were formally dismissed at the end of the three months' trial period. The W.C.T.U., however, renewed the attack and presently there was set up under civil service regulations a class of "boarding matrons," who were to board the liners and assist the male inspectors. Williams was carefully instructed to select from the eligible lists "those who are found to be kindhearted, who have tact and good judgment, and who will appreciate the position they occupy and not presume upon the authority vested in them." They were to act in an advisory capacity only, "leaving the final determination of all doubtful matters to the judgment of the boarding inspectors."[9]

The European crusade against what had come to be called the White Slave Trade ("la traite des blanches") had gathered strength over the years. Starting from a private base, primarily in England, it had eventually drawn in most of the governments. There had been an international congress in 1902, held at the invitation of the French government, to consider what could be done to check "the abominable traffic in girls for immoral purposes." The feminist reformer, Josephine Butler, had started the agitation in England many years before, in a revolt against the double standard as expressed in British law designed to protect the armed forces from venereal disease. It had been dramatized by William T. Stead, editor of the *Pall Mall Gazette,* and aided by one or two senior British statesmen. The objectionable British legislation had finally been repealed, over violent opposition, but the crusade had meanwhile spread to the Continent. It soon came under the leadership of William Alexander Coote and the English National Vigilance Association.

Mr. Coote had become convinced that a vast international organization was at work recruiting girls under false promises over much of Europe, particularly in the poorer countries, for the houses of prostitution of Western Europe, Asia, and South Africa. Coote shared this view with the German Socialist writer, August Bebel, and may have been influenced by him. Bebel's work on the subject of women in history was translated and published in London in 1885, shortly after it had first appeared. Bebel traced the history of woman's place in society, with particular emphasis on prostitution, from Biblical times. He saw no hope of equality for women short of Socialism. In nineteenth century bourgeois Europe, he declared, "the trade in Women's Flesh" had "assumed enormous dimensions." The traffic from European lands was world wide, and was "carried on with an admirable organization, on a most extensive scale, without attracting the attention of the police, in the midst of all our culture and civilization." Backed by wealthy Englishmen, Coote had worked indefatigably and convinced social and political leaders in much of Europe of the reality and great scope of the traffic. Committees had been formed on a national and then on an international basis; a conference of such committees in London in 1889 had preceded the official congress in Paris three years later.[10]

The main outlines of a proposed treaty for the suppression of the White Slave Trade were framed at the Paris congress, but it was decided to allow another two years for the several governments to study the matter further. At the adjourned congress, in May 1904, representatives of thirteen European states signed the treaty. Other states adhered to it later. The principal articles of the treaty called for the establishment or designation of an authority in each signatory state to centralize information on the international traffic in women and girls, and to correspond directly with similar agencies in the other countries; for supervision by each signatory state over railway stations and ports of embarkation to detect procurers and victims of the traffic; and for the notification of the governments of the persons involved, the victims to be held in institutions for return to their country of origin. The United States, though invited, had not sent an official delegation to either session of the congress, and neither of them was noticed in the New York metropolitan press. When the treaty went into effect among the twelve European states that had ratified it, in 1905, the story appeared only briefly on an inside page of the *Times*. There was no great interest in the matter, which the American newspapers seem to have thought of as a purely European problem.[11]

But the Bureau of Immigration was fully aware that the traffic did exist, whether highly organized or not, that it was increasing, and that it extended to the United States. One of the problems of the immigration authorities was that under existing law a woman automatically became a citizen on the naturalization of her husband. Among other devices, women of doubtful character were brought in under certified copies of their husbands' naturalization papers. The marriage might be real or fictitious, or the naturalization papers themselves might be fraudulent. The Commissioner General called attention to this in his 1904 report, though he laid more stress on the problem of diseased immigrants and did not mention White Slavery as such. Beginning in that year, with the law of 1903 in effect, immigration inspectors had begun to bar procurers as well as prostitutes, but only a few of them were spotted and excluded in that year or the next. More prostitutes had also been identified and excluded, the number rising to 24 in 1905.

NOTES

[1] New York *Sun*, November 21, 1902.

[2] New York *Evening Post*, November 21, 1902.

[3] *Ibid.*

[4] *New York Times*, November 22, 1902; *New York Tribune*, November 22, 1902; *Sun*, November 22, 1902; *The American Hebrew*, LXXII (November 28, 1902), 43.

[5] *Annual Report of the Superintendent of Immigration*, 1894, 31-32; *Annual Report of the Commissioner-General of Immigration*, 1896, 15, 17-18; *Ibid.*, 1897, 7-8; *Congressional Record*, 57th Cong., 1st Sess., 5757, 5764, 5813-5835, 5985-6014.

[6] Mary Earhart, *Frances Willard: From Prayers to Politics* (Chicago, 1944), 184-187; Lydia J. Trowbridge, *Frances Willard of Evanston* (Chicago, 1938), 124-125; *Tribune*, January 13, 1903.

[7] *Times*, January 15, 25, 1903; *Tribune*, January 13, 21, 22, 27, February 4, 1903; New York *World*, January 27, 1903.

[8] *Times*, February 12, 1903; *Tribune*, February 17, March 11, 13, 1903.

[9] *Times*, March 14, April 27, October 7, 1903; *Tribune*, May 16, December 30, 1903; Commissioner-General Frank P. Sargent to Commissioner Williams, July 29, 1903, Letters Sent, Press Copies ("Immigration") 1891-1912, Record Group 85, National Archives.

10 Anna G. Spencer, "Josephine Butler and the English Crusade," *Forum,* XLIX (June 1913), 703-716, L (July 1913), 77-81; "The White Slave Trade," *Contemporary Review,* LXXXII (November 1902), 735-740; Thomas Keith, "The Double Standard," *Journal of the History of Ideas,* XX (April 1959), 199; William Burgess, *The World's Social Evil* (Chicago, c. 1914), 115, 241-242, 280-282; William A. Coote, ed., *A Romance of Philanthropy: Being a Record of the Principal Incidents Connected with the Exceptionally Successful Thirty Years' Work of the National Vigilance Association* (London, 1916), 170-180; Ferdinand August Bebel, *Woman in the Past, Present and Future* (London, 1885), 98-100.

11 Committee of Fifteen on the Social Evil, *The Social Evil, with special reference to conditions existing in the City of New York* (2nd edition, New York, 1912), 201-202; *Charities,* IX (October 4, 1902), 326; Burgess, *The World's Social Evil,* 242-243; *Times,* July 18, 1905.

II

The whole problem of immigration, which was rising to flood proportions in these years, was discussed at great length in a conference held at Madison Square Garden in New York in December, 1905, under the auspices of the National Civic Federation. There was much restrictionist sentiment expressed by delegates, who came from 40 states, but White Slavery was not once mentioned in the accounts of the conference, nor in the resolutions adopted at its close. Nevertheless, Commissioner Robert Watchorn, who had succeeded Williams at Ellis Island, a few weeks later expressed concern at the traffic. New York City was now the center of the White Slave traffic of the world, he told newsmen. "Many Hebrews, Italians and Frenchmen come over here to earn a living in a criminal way, sending back for young women," he said. "The women are well drilled on the other side and when they get here know enough to say that the men who meet them are relatives, sometimes their brothers." He had been impressed by the case of one Anatol Harchaux, recently sentenced in the U. S. Circuit Court to a year in the penitentiary. Harchaux had passed through the Port of New York in January, he and one Julia Paureux arriving on the *Lorraine* separately but heading west together. Julia had been arrested in Pueblo, Colorado, on prostitution charges, and Harchaux, who had American citizen's papers, had married her. This gave her immunity from deportation, but the Ellis Island authorities had had the immigration inspector in Denver investigate the case. Harchaux had been arrested and sent back to New York. He had been convicted only a few days before. Women were arriving on every incoming steamer, Watchorn believed, and were being taken to different cities and to Panama. The girls got past the immigration inspectors under false statements, and the authorities at Ellis Island sometimes learned of their arrest only a few weeks later. His office was powerless to stop the traffic, and the only remedy he could suggest was to increase the penalty.[1]

Alien prostitutes were no novelty in New York. Dr. William Sanger, resident physician at the city hospital on Blackwell's Island, had in the 1850's conducted a survey and questionnaire of prostitutes in the city. This was done with the help of the police, and all recognized houses of prostitution were canvassed. Of 2,000 prostitutes listed, 1238 were found to have been born abroad. Thousands more were known to be operating independently. They were chiefly Irish, German, and British girls, reflecting the dominant sources of immigration in the period. The higher-priced "parlor houses," Sanger found, were filled with native American girls. He did not believe that prostitution could ever be eradicated, but he was concerned over the spread of venereal disease and favored the policy then general in Europe of registering, segregating, and periodically examining prostitutes. "In this Western hemisphere," he noted, "and in the mother-country, Anglo-Saxon prudery has stood aloof from inquiring into a vice which every one admits to be offensive to the moral sense of the people, and has submitted to an accumulation of evils rather than seek to abate them." He made no serious inquiry into how immigrant girls were recruited into the profession, though he did mention the "malign influences" of ports of departure, the swindling of boarding-house keepers, the "intrigues of an intelligence-office," and "the wiles of abandoned ones of their own sex" as contributing factors. Diplomatically, since he had to depend on them for his basic data, he made no mention of how much the police might be collecting in graft for permitting the madame to operate their illegal houses.[2]

French prostitutes became conspicuous in New York with the 1870's. The Parisian "maquereau" (mackerel), or pimp, who had thrived in the pleasure-loving regime of Napoleon III, was less tolerated under the succeeding republic. The type began to emigrate in considerable numbers, taking their girls with them and sending back home for fresh faces from time to time. New York, where control of prostitution consisted largely of police tolerance in exchange for tribute, tempered by occasional arrests and raids to appease the public and keep the payments coming in, offered a highly profitable outlet for their business. The area centering on Sixth Avenue and 33rd Street was developing into a concentration of gambling houses, houses of prostitution, shady hotels, and low saloons and dance halls, nationally notorious. It came to be called the "Tenderloin," as it offered the choicest graft to senior police officers assigned to it. By 1880, when Max F. Schmittberger, a young policeman, was assigned to the precinct, he testified years later, "French women used to stand out in front of the railing in front of their houses and pull every man in as he went through the street. When citizens complained, they got no satisfaction," When, in 1892, the Reverend Charles H. Parkhurst, president of the Society for the Prevention of Crime, began denouncing from his pulpit the Tammany Democratic administration and its police for protecting vice, he was challenged to prove his charges. He thereupon hired a private detective to take him on a tour of the underworld. A number of the places they visited, in the Tenderloin and in Greenwich Village, were filled with lively French girls. At one house, for a price, they were treated to a "French Circus," which neither Parkhurst nor his guide was willing to describe in detail later. Parkhurst's crusade continued, and in 1894 brought about the temporary defeat of Tammany. At the hearings of the Lexow Committee, investigating the Police Department before the election, one of the principal witnesses was Mrs. Matilda Herman, known as the "French Madame." She managed four houses and employed twenty-five girls. Over a period of only a few years, she testified, she had paid the police more than $30,000 for protection. The police had kidnapped her and smuggled her out of town for a time to try to prevent her from testifying.[3]

NOTES

[1] *Annual Report of the Commissioner-General of Immigration, 1904,* 105-106, 129; *Ibid.,* 1905, 10; "The National Conference on Immigration," *National Civic Federation Review,* II (January-February 1906), 1-6, 14-19; *Evening Post,* December 5-8, 1905; *Times,* December 6-8, 23, 1905; *World,* December 6-7, 23, 1905.

2 William W. Sanger, M.D., *The History of Prostitution: Its Extent, Causes, and Effects Throughout the World* (New York, 1859), 19-20, 33-34, 460-461; Clifford G. Roe, *The Great War on White Slavery; or, Fighting for the Protection of our Girls* (n. p., c. 1911), 205-207.

3 Gustavus Myers, "Tammany and Vice," *The Independent,* LII (December 1900), 2926; George Kibbe Turner, "The Daughters of the Poor," *McClure's Magazine,* XXXIV (November 1909), 46-47; Lloyd R. Morris, *Incredible New York: High Life and Low Life of the Last Hundred Years* (New York, 1951), 111-112; William T. Stead, *Satan's Invisible World Displayed; or Despairing Democracy* (New York, 1897), 96, 151-154; Charles W. Gardner, *The Doctor and the Devil, or Midnight Adventure of Dr. Parkhurst* (Reprint edition, New York, 1931), 57-62; Morris R. Werner, *Tammany Hall* (Garden City, 1928), 348-349, 389-392.

III

As the great Jewish immigration from Eastern Europe developed, a new contingent of alien prostitutes appeared. Like every other major migration, this one contained its criminal element. Jewish gamblers, thieves, and procurers quickly adapted themselves to the corrupt political system that controlled the lower East Side, where Jews and Italians were displacing the older Irish and German elements, and formed alliances with the Irish politicians who dominated Tammany Hall. "Silver Dollar" Smith, whose real name seems to have been Charles Solomon, had his famous saloon, its floor paved with silver dollars, opposite the Essex Market Court. Smith did a flourishing business in bailing out prostitutes brought to the Court. He was a prominent member of Tammany Hall, and his saloon served as a rendezvous for the Max Hochstim Association, sometimes known as the Essex Market Court gang. Hochstim's bully boys once mobbed agents of Dr. Parkhurst's society after they emerged from the court, where they had given evidence against disorderly house keepers in the neighborhood. The police of the precinct, then headed by the notorious Captain William (Big Bill) Devery, did not interfere. Martin Engel, the Tammany district leader, was a member of the Max Hochstim Association and evidently directed its operations, though he did not soil his hands in mobbing vice crusaders. As Mary Simkhovitch, then of the College Settlement on Rivington Street, near the heart of the red-light district, testified, "At election time he used to drive through our ward in an open barouche, his fingers laden with diamonds, and more diamonds shone from his cravat." Engel, in turn, owed allegiance to "Big Tim" Sullivan, Tammany boss of the Bowery. Sullivan, as Mrs. Simkhovitch noted, "drew tribute from a whole region."[1]

Pimps formed a good part of the membership of the Max Hochstim Association. They seemed to have recruited their girls at first from mill towns in nearby states, but as their business boomed in the heavily male Jewish district they began preying on their own people. What came to be called the "Cadet System" developed. The cadets, or pimps, increasingly second generation immigrants, recruited unsophisticated "greenhorn" Jewish and other girls on the streets and in dance halls for the flourishing houses of prostitution, shady hotels, and tenement-house brothels. The appalling conditions of vice and crime in the area adjoining the Bowery to the east, which had become known as "*The* Red Light District," furnished much of the ammunition for the Parkhurst crusade and the Lexow Committee. Activities there diminished for a time, after a Fusion party victory, but Tammany returned to power in 1897 and conditions in the Tenderloin and along the Bowery were soon worse than ever. A new wave of reform, spearheaded by the citizens' Committee of Fifteen, turned Tammany out once more in 1901, much of the impetus coming from the exposure of blatant and aggressive prostitution on the lower East Side.

There the respectable Jews who formed the bulk of the population were horrified at the prevailing conditions. As Dr. Morris Behrman, an East Side physician, testified in 1899, "it is pretty hard for us respectable people to sustain ourselves there." Complaint had no effect. "I presume it is because the district is managed from a political rather than from a civic standpoint," said Dr. Behrman. "There is a boss in the district . . . Martin Engel is the boss of the East Side."

The Committee of Fifteen itself was the result of a junction of forces between Jewish groups and the Episcopal Church. Bishop Henry Codman Potter, of the Diocese of New York, had written a public letter to Mayor Robert Van Wyck, the tool of Tammany, after one of the Bishop's missionaries on the East Side had gone to the local police precinct, and then to the district inspector, to complain of the open vice in the district, and been "met with insolent derision." Vice there, Potter told Van Wyck and the world at large, took the form of "a rapacious licentiousness which stops at no outrages and spares no tenderest victim. Such a state of things cries to God for vengeance, and calls no less loudly to you and me for redress." Isador Straus, president of the Educational Alliance on the East Side, at the same time made a personal appeal to Richard Croker, the Tammany boss, and his assembled chieftains. The charge had been made, he said, that the greater part of the revenue of Tammany Hall was from "the people in evil conditions of life and that no good could be accomplished in this city unless the power of Tammany Hall was destroyed." He was himself a Democrat, and this charge had been thrown up to him time and again.

Croker hastily appointed a committee of his own, "to stamp out vice and crime in New York," and departed to Europe for his health. Croker's committee, after a few highly publicized gestures at reform, was dissolved under pressure from Big Tim Sullivan. The Committee of Fifteen, on the other hand, in alliance with a variety of reform groups, made a thorough study of vice and gambling in New York City under the Tammany administration, carried on prosecutions, issued devastating reports, and was largely reponsible for the downfall of Tammany in the election of 1901. Its efforts were aided greatly by Jerome's crusading campaign for district attorney, which he centered on the Jewish East Side.[2]

While Jewish procurers appear to have recruited largely among unsophisticated girls already landed in the United States, and the French to have depended on the importation of professionals, there was active Jewish participation in the White Slave trade in the original sense of an international traffic. French accounts of the traffic throughout Europe tended to stress Eastern Jewish dominance, and there was obvious anti-Semitism in the growing American literature on the subject, but there was substance in such material. The vice raids in Philadelphia had dramatized a real traffic conducted largely by Jewish procurers. Some, if not all, of these had come from New York, taking refuge from the furor roused by the Committee of Fifteen and the Low reform administration that followed. These men unquestionably did some importing. Some of them fled the country when a wave of reform struck Philadelphia, operating in South Africa and elsewhere until they felt it safe to return. Others transferred their operations to distant cities across the United States, keeping their New York connections and getting their girls largely from there. These girls may have been largely recruited in the city by cadets after their arrival, but direct importation was a factor in the trade. The National Council of Jewish Women, which had its agent at Ellis Island, paid particular attention to the problem among the steerage immigrants landed there. But none of the numerous missionary societies represented there were permitted to operate on the ships, and importers of all nationalities favored cabin passage for their female merchandise to escape close scrutiny at the island.[3]

NOTES

[1] Frank Moss, *The American Metropolis* (3 vols., New York, 1897), III, 164-167, 235-236, 237-240; Werner, *Tammany Hall,* 354-355, 380-382, 438-439; Turner, "Daughters of the Poor," 47; Mary Kingsbury Simkhovitch, *Neighborhood* (New York, 1938), 64-65.

[2] George Kibbe Turner, "Tammany's Control of New York by Professional Criminals," *McClure's Magazine,* XXIII (June 1909), 120-121; Rev. John P. Peters, "The Story of the Committee of Fourteen of New York," *Social Hygiene,* IV (July 1918), 356-357; Jeremy P. Felt, "Vice Reform as a Political Technique: The Committee of Fifteen in New York, 1900-1901," *New York History,* LIV (January 1973), 27-28, 30-31, 33-34, 36, 38-48, 50-51; *The American Hebrew,* LXIX (November 1, 1901), 618; Committee of Fifteen, *Preliminary Statement* (New York, April 10, 1901), 3-4; *Ibid., The Social Evil; with Special Reference to Conditions Existing in the City of New York* (New York, 1902), Preface; Moses Rischin, *The Promised City: New York's Jews 1870-1914* (New York, 1964), 90, 91, 228; Werner, *Tammany Hall,* 401-402, 470- 471, 473; *Times,* November 16, 17, 18, 25, 28, 1900, November 6, 1901.

[3] "Importing Women for Immoral Purposes," Senate Document 196, 61st Cong., 2d Sess., 23-24; Rene Labaut, "La Traite des Blanches," *La Revue Philanthropique,* XI (Mai a Octobre 1902), 143-144; Turner, "Daughters of the Poor," 48-52; Egal Feldman, "Prostitution, the Alien Woman and the Progressive Imagination, 1910-1915," *American Quarterly,* XIX (Summer 1967), 202-204; Lincoln Steffens, *The Shame of the Cities* (Reprint, New York, 1948), 218-219; Philip Cowen, *Memories of an American Jew* (New York, 1932), 169-170; Arthur A. Goren, *New York Jews and the Quest for Community: The Kehillah Experiment, 1908-1922* (New York, 1970), 134; *Sun,* October 30, 1909.

IV

The great wave of Italian immigration followed and accompanied the Jewish. Italian colonies appeared in different parts of New York City, but the greatest concentration developed alongside that of the Jews on the lower East Side. More often even than was the case with the Jews, Italian immigrants were men coming alone. They furnished much of the unskilled labor force on widely-dispersed construction projects, and tended to return to the district during slack seasons. They formed a booming market for female companionship. Abetted by local Tammany chiefs, Italian pimps set out to satisfy it. Writing about 1900 for the U.S. Industrial Commission, Kate H. Claghorn reviewed the situation that had developed on the lower East Side in recent years. Living in crowded tenements, Hebrews and Italians alike were thrown in with "the corrupt remnants of Irish immigration." The Bowery, with the Italians on one side and the Hebrews on the other, was "the focal line" of the evil influences that had developed under the existing administration. "Until within a very few years," Miss Claghorn stated, "the Italian laboring population in New York was notably free from glaring vice and intemperance. There were few or no disorderly resorts for Italians, and such practice as the importation of Italian women for immoral purposes was unknown." Under existing conditions in the city, however, "positive inducements having been given for the extension of vice of all kinds, many disorderly resorts have been opened in their most crowded quarters, and it is said that many Italian girls from Naples and other cities have been imported to fill them."[1]

Italian pimps, or cadets, operated in much the same way as did Jews of the same type, in contiguous and overlapping territory. They probably got more recruits from immigrant girls of various nationalities recently landed than they imported, but they did import. Matrons at Ellis Island watched carefully for Italian prostitutes. Broughton Brandenburg, a writer returning from Europe in steerage with Italian immigrants in 1903, passed through the inspection line and noticed a "stern-looking" matron looking for "any whose moral character might be questioned." She questioned closely each party as to the various relationships of the men and women in it. "Her Italian was good," Brandenburg noticed.[2] As with the French and the Jews, professional Italian prostitutes probably came most often in cabin class and escaped this rigorous inspection. But young girls accompanied in the steerage or met by young men whom they fervently identified as their brothers or cousins could escape even the eagle eye of the matron at the island.

Paul Kelly, whose real name was Paolo Antonini Vacarelli, was the leader of the Five Pointers, probably the most powerful of the gang on the lower East Side in the early 1900's. Serving Tammany on election day by "repeater" voting and intimidation of the opposition, he and his gang were given a free hand for varied illegal and criminal activities. His principal source of revenue seems to have been a string of cheap houses of prostitution for Italians, and he was credited with having employed from 750 to 1000 women. As Italian mothers in New York guarded their daughters with great care, importation was a necessity. The usual method appears to have been to commission young Italian laborers returning home for a visit, who would persuade young peasant girls to come to America with them under promise of marriage. On arrival, the girls would be turned over to the dealers for the price of passage and a small bonus. The girls might later be shifted to other cities with a growing Italian population, such as Philadelphia, Pittsburgh, Chicago, or Boston.[3]

NOTES

[1] Kate H. Claghorn, "The Foreign Immigrant in New York City," U.S. Industrial Commission, *Reports,* XV, *Immigration and Education* (Washington, 1902), 478.

[2] Broughton Brandenburg, *Imported Americans: The story of the experiences of a disguised American and his wife studying the immigration question* (New York, 1904), 222.

[3] Turner, "Tammany's Control of New York," 123-125; *Ibid.,* "Daughters of the Poor," 57-58. There is a detailed account of Paul Kelly and his chief rival, Monk Eastman, who also engaged in the business of prostitution in the neighboring Jewish Quarter, in Herbert Asbury, *The Gangs of New York: An Informal History of the Underworld* (New York, 1928), 252-296.

V

As a new immigration law began to shape up in 1906, including a number of additional restrictions, the only provision relating to prostitution at first was one proposed by Commissioner Watchorn of Ellis Island. This broadened the exclusion of prostitutes by extending it to "women or girls coming in the United States for the purpose of prostitution, or for any other immoral purpose." This was directed primarily against female procurers and house madams, but was later applied to private mistresses as well. An amendment extending to three years the period during which alien prostitutes, procurers, and criminals might be deported was later agreed to without debate. The problem of foreign prostitution was recognized and the bars against it were being raised, but there was no suggestion of a crusade on the subject. There was no reference to the White Slave Trade by name. The annual report of the Commissioner-General of Immigration made no mention of foreign prostitutes and procurers as a special problem, though its tabulations showed a slight increase in rejections of these classes. As the immigration bill moved to passage in the following session of Congress, debate centered mainly on a proposed literacy test, Japanese exclusion, and other matters, but the language on the subject of alien prostitution was strengthened. Penalties were added to apply to anyone who should hold or attempt to hold an alien prostitute or should "keep, maintain, control, support or harbor" her within three years after she entered the United States. The problem was recognized, but there was no great alarm.[1]

The White Slave Trade was not yet a matter of great national concern, but events were rapidly shaping up to make it such. William Coote, whose fervid warnings and appeals throughout Europe had been largely responsible for the international congresses of 1902 and 1904, had made several attempts "to focus the attention of the American people on the Suppression of the White Slave Traffic," and to urge the formation in the United States of a national vigilance committee along the lines of the British organization that he headed. In 1906 a group of social workers and reformers concerned with the problem of prostitution, generally referred to as "The Social Evil," began forming such an organization. They invited him to visit the United States and help them, guaranteeing his expenses. Coote was a zealot and had no doubt of direct inspiration from God in his work. He accepted the call as "a remarkable intervention of Providence," arriving early in the following year. In New York, Washington, Philadelphia, Baltimore, and Boston, he met with private groups and held public meetings, and "was able to arouse much interest in the hearts and minds of the people," as he recorded later. There were numerous organizations in the United States, some of long standing, generally sympathetic to his views, and it was not long before a National Vigilance Committee appeared, soon followed by vigilance committees in many states. These organizations made war on sexual vice in general, the term White Slavery being quickly expanded to cover the whole field.

It was equated with commercialized vice and applied to the strictly domestic traffic as well as to the international, but the tendency was to blame foreigners for both. These committees and their allies sponsored most of the repressive legislation on the subject that proliferated on the state statute books in the years that followed, and they soon made themselves felt at the national level.[2]

NOTES

[1] *Congressional Record,* 59th Cong., 1st Sess., 7212-7234, 7284-7300, 9158-9195; *Ibid.,* 2d Sess., 2808-2817, 2939-2952, 3017-3039, 3083-3099, 3210-3232; *Annual Report of the Commissioner-General of Immigration,* 1906, 7, 69-72; *Times,* February 14, 1909.

[2] Coote, *A Romance of Philanthropy,* 180-181; Committee of Fifteen, *The Social Evil* (1912 ed.), 207-208; Anna G. Spencer, "A World Crusade," *Forum,* L (August 1913), 194; Roy Lubove, "The Progressive and the Prostitute," *Historian,* XXIV (May 1962), 308-309.

VI

More important than Coote's missionary work in stimulating this sort of activity was a sensational exposé of vice conditions in Chicago. While the muckraking periodicals that flourished in the early twentieth century had devoted a good bit of attention to political corruption in the cities and in the national government, it was not until 1907 that any of them took up the subject of vice dramatically. In the April issue of *McClure's Magazine* appeared George Kibbe Turner's "The City of Chicago," and probably the most notable crusade of the Progressive period was launched. Turner, who was on the magazine's staff, set out to describe the seamy side of life in the nation's second city, starting with the liquor traffic. Next he turned to "the second great business of dissipation — prostitution." He estimated that there were at least 10,000 professional prostitutes in the city, and that the revenues from the business in 1906 amounted to over $20,000,000. The women were badly exploited and received only a small share of their earnings. English-speaking girls were recruited by professional pimps among the low paid employees of the department stores and factories. "The largest regular business in furnishing women, however," Turner declared, "is done by a company of men, largely composed of Russian Jews, who supply women of that nationality to the trade. These men have a sort of loosely organized association extending through the large cities of the country, their chief centers being New York, Boston, Chicago, and New Orleans." In Chicago they now furnished the great majority of the prostitutes in the cheaper West Side Levee district, and their women had driven out the English-speaking women in the last ten years. They were closely allied with such local Democratic bosses as "Hinky-Dink" McKenna and "Bath-House John" Coughlin.[1]

Clifford G. Roe, state's attorney in Cook County, had already begun prosecuting White Slave cases vigorously under such legislation as existed, and quite likely furnished much information to Turner on vice conditions in Chicago. *McClure's Magazine* followed up Turner's dramatic exposé in the next issue with an article composed entirely of extracts from Chicago newspapers, "Chicago as Seen by Herself." A number of areas of sin and depravity were described. The district known as the West Side Levee, in particular, was depicted as a "public Emporium of immorality and degradation," which existed by virtue of a regularly organized "protective association" whose members laughed at the law and, through some mysterious influence, were enabled to continue their traffic with "a license and abandon that makes of the West Side Levee an open brothel." In the following year, under such stimulus, the Illinois Vigilance Association was formed to fight White Slavery in the state. In Chicago the Joint Club Committee was organized "for the suppression of the traffic in girls," and Roe was made chairman. Leaders of the Jewish community, stung by Turner's charges, were particularly active in it. This committee, which included leading judges and lawyers in the city, brought about the passage of the Illinois Pandering Law, directed against the professional procurer, which was later copied

18

in other states. Another Chicago group, the Immigrants' Protective League, was also formed at this time under the leadership of Grace Abbott of the Hull House Settlement and Judge Julian Mack, prominent in the Jewish community. The League devoted much of its attention to protecting immigrant girls, arriving alone in the city from Ellis Island, against the wiles of the White Slavers.[2]

The Bureau of Immigration was put on the defensive by the wave of publicity and indignation that followed Turner's article, and sought to justify itself. The Commissioner-General's annual report for the fiscal year 1907 for the first time discussed the White Slave traffic by name and at length. The importation of women and girls for immoral purposes, it pointed out, had been one of the first of the "immigration evils" to engage the attention of Congress and had been prohibited by law as early as 1875. With the growth of immigration, and with the improved law of 1903, "no small part of the duties of the service has consisted in trying to prevent the importation and to effect the deportation of such persons and their procurers." It was believed, rather optimistically, that the traffic had been diminished in recent years because of the European crusade, but much remained to be done. The new immigration law was a decided improvement, "and places in the hands of the Bureau a measure with which it hopes to make an energetic and effective fight." A further measure was suggested: qualified women with a knowledge of foreign languages should be selected and appointed to serve on the vessels of the larger steamship lines, to mingle with the foreign women and gather data which could be placed before the boards of special inquiry at Ellis Island. Not much could be done in this way by the boarding matrons in the brief period after a liner left Quarantine headed for its pier on the North River.[3]

The Commissioner-General's promise to use the new law aggressively was not mere bureaucratic double talk. The burden of enforcement, though a nation-wide problem, fell most heavily on the Ellis Island authorities, whose immediate jurisdiction included New York City and much of New Jersey. A story given out in Washington announced that the Bureau of Immigration was going to make a systematic effort "to put an end to the white slave trade which, it is asserted, has been conducted especially in cities on the Atlantic seaboard for a long time." Women immigrant inspectors were now authorized for the principal ports, and, on Commissioner Watchorn's recommendation, Helen M. Bullis was appointed at Ellis Island. Miss Bullis was one of the social workers who had invited Coote to come to the United States and help form a national vigilance committee. There was no doubt of her zeal in the new assignment, which involved personal investigation in the Tenderloin. A departmental circular followed, calling the attention to all immigration officers of the new legal provisions and directing active search for alien prostitutes and procurers who might be deported under the three-year clause. Secretary of Commerce and Labor Oscar S. Straus, under whom the Bureau of Immigration operated, had recently made a trip through the northwestern and Pacific Coast states. He had found not only that hundreds of Japanese women were being imported, but that there was importation of "women from France, Austria, Russia, and Italy."[4]

NOTES

1 George Kibbe Turner, "The City of Chicago," *McClure's Magazine*, XXVIII (April 1907), 580-584; Louis Filler, *Crusaders for American Liberalism* (Yellow Springs, 1950), 288-289; Lubove, "The Progressive and the Prostitute," 312-313.

2 "Chicago as Seen by Herself," *McClure's Magazine*, XXVIX (May 1907), 69; Roe, *The Great War on White Slavery*, 190-192; Henry B. Leonard, "The Immigrants' Protective League of Chicago, 1908-1921," *Journal of the Illinois State Historical Society*, LXVI (Autumn 1973), 276-277.

3 *Annual Report of the Commissioner-General of Immigration*, 1907, 63-64.

4 *Times*, August 30, October 5, 1907; *Evening Post*, October 4, 1907; Department Circular No. 156, Bureau of Immigration and Naturalization, Sept. 26, 1907, in "Suppression of the White-Slave Traffic," Senate Document 214, 61st Cong., 2d Sess.

VII

In New York City a Committee of Fourteen had succeeded the Committee of Fifteen to carry on its work. The special target of the new committee was the so-called "Raines Law Hotel," which was licensed to serve drinks on Sunday and was usually a thinly-disguised brothel. Immigration authorities and the Committee of Fourteen now brought pressure on the Police Department. Tammany was in power again, after a two-year Fusion reform administration, but Mayor George B. McClellan, Jr., had shown some independence. He had, after his reelection in 1905, appointed Theodore A. Bingham, a retired Army officer, as his police commissioner. Bingham was trying to break up the traditional system of corruption that had for generations pervaded the Police Department, reviving quickly after each wave of reform. Considerable publicity had recently been given to charges of police protection to gambling, and Bingham was probably more sensitive to this than to the White Slave problem. Nevertheless, he gave active help and began raiding both kinds of establishments. He often had to use reluctant subordinates, many of whom felt that their primary loyalty was to the permanent Tammany machine rather than to the commissioner or the moment. His control of the department had recently been strengthened by legislation obtained in Albany after a hard fight, and he began making frequent transfers, promotions, and demotions. District Attorney Jerome, not to be outdone, began raiding on his own. The immigration law of 1907 had provided for an Immigration Commission, to study in detail all aspects of the subject and report to Congress. The Commission soon began devoting a good part of its effort to the White Slave Trade, employing a number of secret agents. Large cities across the country were checked, but there was special attention to New York, where the Commission worked closely with both Commissioner Bingham and the immigration authorities at Ellis Island.[1]

The Tenderloin, where most of the more expensive parlor houses and gambling joints were located, became the principal target of all these agencies. Beginning with the fall of 1907, persistent vice and gambling raids and arrests by one or another of them brought general consternation and disarray to the area, though rivalry developed between Bingham and Jerome, both rather flamboyant personalities, and sometimes they got in each other's way. In one spectacular raid, over 800 women were turned out of the houses in the Tenderloin. Most of these women transferred their activities to the back rooms of saloons or Raines Law hotels, to tenement houses or massage parlors, but a good many left the city. The large French contingent was more or less permanently dispersed. The French Club at 124 West 29th Street, to which Immigration Commission agents found much baggage of French men and women arriving from Europe had been manifested, became recognized as a headquarters and distribution center for procurers and was finally closed. Correspondence captured there revealed extensive but loosely organized operations extending from the flesh markets of Paris to New York, Chicago, Seattle, and other American cities. Importation now became more difficult and the local market less profitable. French procurers in numbers left town, taking their girls with them to cities in the West or out of the country. One underworld informant later told Turner that of over 400 Frenchmen whom he knew personnally in the Tenderloin before the 1907 raids, not 100 were active a year or so later. The French maquereaux, unlike their Jewish or Italian rivals, had always retained close links to their homeland, expecting to return there. Many of them never bothered to learn English and they had not become part of the Tammany machine, relying on cash payment alone for protection. When the storm of vice reform broke they were unable to furnish protection to their women driven from the parlor houses into the street. The French element in the Tenderloin melted away, and the district never quite recovered its old-time glow.[2]

It was in 1907, also, that the institution of a night court was set up in New York City, by amendment to the city charter. Most of the arrests of prostitutes were made after the regular magistrates' courts were closed. It was necessary either to hold them all night or release them on bail. This situation led to much graft on the part of professional bondsmen, who bailed out the women and put them back on the street to earn the money to pay for the bond. The new court was designed to break up this system by making bail unnecessary. The police were instructed to send to the night court all cases in which the magistrate had summary jurisdiction and every female prisoner who was not charged with committing a felony. During its investigation of the White Slave traffic in New York City, the Immigration Commission examined all women convicted of prostitution in this court for a period of four months. During this period there were 2,093 such convictions, 581 of them being of foreign-born women — 225 of them Jewish, 154 French, 29 Irish, 26 South Italian, 19 English, 10 Polish, and others scattered. Few of them admitted having arrived within the three-year period making them liable to deportation. Later on, the Immigration Service covered the sessions of the night court systematically, to pick up alien prostitutes subject to deportation. Fiorello La Guardia, afterward mayor of New York City, served for a time as an interpreter in this court.[3]

Police Commissioner Bingham's report for the calendar year 1908 was less than kind to the immigration authorities at Ellis Island. Bingham had numerous problems with alien criminals, and Ellis Island was a convenient scapegoat. The Police Department, he said, had given careful attention to the traffic in importing women for purposes of prostitution, "especially among the French." This traffic was found to be of large dimentions. "There seems to be very slight difficulty in getting women into this country," he asserted, and the requirements of the immigration authorities were "easily met by various simple subterfuges." The men engaged in the traffic seemed to have an organization, or at least an understanding, which was national and even international in scope. The figures, which he cited, on cases brought by the Police Department during the year against alien prostitutes and pimps showed only a small part of what had been accomplished. According to his best information, "a large number of men have taken their women to other cities, and even to other countries, on account of the risk they run by staying in New York." The Ellis

Island people, however, often failed to deport the aliens after they had been rounded up, and would even allow a foreign prostitute to remain in the country if she managed to arrange a marriage with an American citizen. Bingham, who had earlier denounced Immigration Commissioner Watchorn for not deporting Italian Black Hand extortionists whom he had corraled and sent to the island, made no allowance for the niceties of Federal law that bound the immigration officials.[4]

NOTES

[1] Committee of Fourteen, *The Social Evil in New York City: A Study of Law Enforcement* (New York, 1910), 25-26; Samuel Hopkins Adams, "The New York Police Force: A Semi-Secret and Semi-Criminal Organization," *Collier's,* XXXIX (March 30, 1907), 15-17; "Governor Hughes and the Legislature," *American Review of Reviews,* XXXV (May 1907), 524-525; Josiah Flynt (pseud.), "Corporation and Police Partnership with the Criminal Pool-Rooms," *Cosmopolitan,* XLIII (June 1907), 161-168; "Importing Women for Immoral Purposes," 3-4.

[2] Committee of Fourteen, *The Social Evil in New York City,* 27; "Importing Women for Immoral Purposes," 18-19, 26-27, 44; U.S. Immigration Commission, *Reports* (41 vols., Washington, 1911), XXXVII, 59, 70, 83-84; Turner, "Tammany's Control of New York," 127-128; *Herald,* October 3, 30, November 7, December 3, 12, 1907; *Sun,* October 28, 1907; *Times,* November 7, 14, 1907, January 11, 16, 1908; *World,* October 29, 1907.

[3] Committee of Fourteen, *The Social Evil,* 85-86; U.S. Immigration Commission, *Reports,* XXXVII, 62, 64; Fiorello H. LaGuardia, *The Making of an Insurgent: An Autobiography, 1882-1919* (Philadelphia, 1948), 70-71.

[4] *Annual Report of the Police Commissioner, City of New York,* 1908, 20-22.

VIII

The Immigration Commission had begun its study of the White Slave Trade in New York and other American cities in November 1907, collecting most of its data in the following year. The Commission was somewhat critical of the immigration authorities, but more sympathetic to their problems. Close examination of the ships' manifests stored at Ellis Island had revealed that in the past, women who had given addresses at well-known disreputable houses in New York and other cities had been allowed to land. Most of these had come in the second cabin; procurers knew that they would escape the close scrutiny given to steerage immigrants, but were reluctant to spend money for first-class passage and knew that their women might be conspicuous in the first cabin. Much greater care was now being taken by the immigration inspectors, the Commission noted, but it was often extremely difficult to prove the illegal entrance of either prostitutes or procurers. The inspector had to judge mainly by their appearance and the stories they told. Correspondence captured at the French Club showed the care taken by the importers in dressing their women well, in coaching the girls regarding the people to whom they were booked as relatives, and in making their stories match on arrival in New York. An embassassing case of mistaken detention was cited, involving the wife of a prominent American citizen. "If such mistakes were committed frequently," the Commissioner warned, "the service would soon be discredited." Eternal vigilance and vigorous prosecution of the cases found would lessen the extent of the evil; "its absolute eradication is hardly to be expected."[1]

The belief that a vast international organization controlled the White Slave Trade had become widespread since Coote's evangelizing visit to the United States. Even well-informed social workers sometimes accepted it. Frances Kellor, writing for the *Atlantic Monthly* early in 1908, demanded greater protection for immigrant girls who, she said, received adequate protection from the wiles of procurers only when they were actually passing through Ellis Island. Action was called for at both state and national levels. The new immigration law was helpful as far as it went, but "Unfortunately the government does not realize the power of the strongly intrenched syndicate, with its many agents abroad and distributed in the various cities, with large financial backing, which imports immigrant girls and sells them from city to city, and has not provided adequate machinery to reach this all-powerful combine." This belief ran parallel in time to the popular acceptance of the existence of a vast Black Hand criminal organization among the Italians. Both added to the growing hostility to the so-called "new" immigration, especially the Jews and the Italians. Together, in their day, they provided what Thomas Beer called "the demonic shape essential to American journalism."

Settlement workers, however, were most concerned with the well-being of the immigrants themselves. Lillian Wald and her staff at the Henry Street Settlement a little later persuaded Governor Charles Evans Hughes to work for state action toward the general welfare of the immigrant, whom they knew to be exploited in a variety of ways. Legislation was shortly passed in Albany directing the governor to appoint a commission to examine "the condition, welfare and industrial opportunities of aliens in the State of New York." Both Miss Kellor and Miss Wald were made members of the commission. Its investigations were made in 1908 and the first months of the succeeding year. The commission found many devices in use to recruit alien girls into a life of prostitution. "In the State of New York, as in other states and countries of the world," it reported, "there are organized, ramified and well-equipped associations to secure girls for the purpose of prostitution." Its attention had been called to one organization incorporated under the laws of New York State as a mutual benefit society, but actually "an association of gamblers, procurers, and keepers of disorderly houses, organized for the purpose of mutual protection in their business." It had a membership of about one hundred in New York City, a good number of whom were engaged in importation. It had representatives and correspondents in many cities, notably Pittsburgh, Chicago, and San Francisco. This report did not give this organization a name, but it was soon to receive a vast amount of publicity and to be identified as a Jewish group.[2]

The annual report of the Commissioner-General of Immigration for 1908 indicated that during the past year there had been "great activity" in "the suppression of the importation of alien women for purposes of prostitution." Rejections at the ports had increased several fold, and there had been quite a number of deportations, including both prostitutes and procurers. Numerous prosecutions had been brought against alien procurers and keepers of houses of ill-fame, and a number of convictions had been obtained. "It is highly necessary," said the Commissioner-General, warming up to the subject, "that this diabolical traffic, which has attained international proportions, should be dealt with in a manner adequate to compass its suppression." Toward this end the time limit on deportation of this class should be removed.

Ellis Island had so many foreign prostitutes in detention at this time, awaiting hearings or deportation, that they were becoming a problem. They were mostly cabin class passengers and had to be detained in the same limited quarters with other detained cabin class women, many of them with teenage daughters. This was a "deplorable state of affairs," the Commissioner reported to Washington. While there had been convictions of a number of procurers and keepers of houses of ill-fame under the law passed the year before, it was noted, there was difficulty in fixing the date of arrival, alien prostitutes usually claiming that they had been in the country more than three years. If they could establish this, they were still immune from deportation. Special instructions had gone to the field, putting the burden of proof on the prostitute that she had been in the country long enough to give her immunity.[3]

Commissioner Watchorn at Ellis Island encountered special difficulty in this connection. A clever, energetic male immigration inspector named Andrew Tedesco had been added to the staff to specialize in White Slave investigations in New York City, supplementing the work of Inspectress Helen Bullis. Tedesco reported an organized racket at work in the Tenderloin, in which data were sold to procurers and prostitutes establishing an early landing date for them.

The Washington office pointed out that the gang working the racket could hardly operate without connivance of someone having access to the records at Ellis Island. The ships' manifests, with space for 30 names on a sheet, carried detailed information on every immigrant landed, and copies of these remained on the island as the basis for most statistics on immigration. There were often blank spaces on the manifest sheets, and these could be filled in with fictitious data. Watchorn was instructed to conduct a quiet investigation so as not to alarm the culprits. Meanwhile, he was to have his boards of special inquiry sitting on such cases to watch carefully for suspicious claims of early landing and investigate them carefully before accepting them.[4]

The Paris treaty of 1904, calling for international cooperation in stamping out the trade in women, had been approved by the Senate, but had not been proclaimed, apparently because it called for enforcement by national police, and the United States had no such institution. President Roosevelt had been using the Secret Service freely for varied criminal investigations, but he was encountering opposition and Congress was soon to put a stop to it. (This situation, incidentally, created a vacuum later filled by the Federal Bureau of Investigation.) The National Vigilance Committee now brought pressure to bear on the Administration, reinforcing reports of investigations conducted by the Bureau of Immigration abroad, indicating a flourishing traffic in women between Europe and both North and South American ports. Secretary of State Elihu Root became convinced that the treaty could be made operative by cooperation between the Federal and state governments, and the President proclaimed it as in effect on June 15, 1908. Under this treaty the Commissioner-General of Immigration was designated as the authority to centralize all information on the international traffic and authorized to correspond directly with imilar services in the signatory powers.[5]

This treaty did not prove to be very effective, as far as the United States was concerned. The Commissioner-General of Immigration reported in the following year that there had not been "any great degree of success in handling this matter by cooperation." The Bureau of Immigration had tried to establish working relations with overseas police authorities, but the response had not been very enthusiastic. The Commissioner-General tried to reason out the failure as a difference in moral attitude:

> Europe is a field in which 'white slaves' are recruited by the human demons who seduce or buy the girls; the United States is a field in which they are sold or farmed out, but as a general rule they are not brought here until they have become confirmed prostitutes. Moreover, the term 'white slave' as generally employed and understood in European countries does not mean nearly so much as the expression 'prostitute' or 'immoral woman' which appears in the United States statute. The purpose of the white-slave agreement is to prevent the seduction of and traffic in innocent girls; the prupose of the immigration act is to prevent the introduction into the United States not only of innocent girls who have been seduced into a life of prostitution, but of all girls and women of sexually immoral class.

The acting secretary of the Department of Commerce and Labor, writing to the Secretary of State in review of the situation, said that "experience has demonstrated that little cooperation can be expected by this country . . . in the enforcement of the United States statute." The objectives of the European convention and the American law were not the same.

While the treaty did not seem to be producing much in the way of cooperation, the Bureau of Immigration was active on the domestic front. In planning its special effort "toward ridding the country of alien prostitutes and procurers," the Commissioner-General reported, it had directed Inspector Marcus Braun early in the fiscal year to make general investigations covering all of the largest cities of the United States. From his reports and the follow-up campaign, the Bureau was "satisfied that an enormous business is constantly being transacted in the importation and distribution of foreign women for purposes of prostitution." It had not been able to discover "any direct or positive evidence of the existence of a combination or syndicate for the transaction of this nefarious busines." There was, however, "a certain esprit de corps" among its practitioners, and in some of the larger cities there were regularly established clubs and headquarters where these men congregated. In some places wealthy leaders had emerged among them, and in certain cities the traffic was "more or less connected with local political conditions." The police and other municipal authorities were "either implicated or else helpless to assist in even the partial eradication of the evil."[6]

NOTES

[1] U. S. Immigration Commission, *Reports*, XXXVII,59, 69-70, 71, 73.

[2] Frances A. Kellor, "The Protection of Immigrant Women," *Atlantic Monthly*, CI (February 1908), 246-255; Thomas Beer, *The Mauve Decade* (Reprint, New York, 1961), 44; Lillian Wald, *The House on Henry Street* (New York, 1915), 293-294; Allen F. Davis, *Spearheads for Reform: The Social Settlements and the Progressive Movement, 1890-1914* (New York, 1967), 94; *Report of the Commission of Immigration of the State of New York* (Albany, 1909), 16-17.

[3] *Annual Report of the Commissioner-General of Immigration*, 1908, 123-124, 217-218; Commissioner Watchorn to Commissioner-General Sargent, June 9, 1908, File 52/519/18, General Immigration Files, Record Group 85, National Archives.

[4] Assistant Secretary Wheeler to Commissioner, Ellis Island (Confidential), March 3, 1909, Letters Sent, Press Copies, ("Immigration") 1891-1912, Record Group 85, National Archives; La Guardia, *The Making of an Insurgent*, 74.

[5] Committee of Fifteen, *The Social Evil* (1912 ed.), 207-208; Clifford G. Roe, *Panders and Their White Slaves* (New York, 1910), 208-209; *Annual Report of the Commissioner-General of Immigration*, 1908, 124-125, 217-218.

[6] *Annual Report of the Commissioner-General of Immigration*, 1909, 116-117; Ormsby McHarg, Acting Secretary of Commerce and Labor, to Secretary of State, October 23, 1909, in "Suppression of the White Slave Traffic."

IX

The United States district attorneys, especially in New York and Chicago, had been using the 1907 law vigorously against alien procurers and house madams, working with the agents of the Bureau of Immigration and the Immigration Commission, and with local volunteer organizations. In Chicago there was little help from the police, and in New York the police commissioner was severely handicapped by Tammany influence. This promising campaign now received a sharp check. In April 1909 the Supreme Court, in the cases of U.S. vs. Keller and U.S. vs. Ullman, with several justices dissenting, held that that part of the law relating to the "harboring" of prostitutes was unconstitutional. The control and abatement of houses of prostitution were held to be strictly within the police powers reserved to the states. The decision practically brought to an end, for the time being, Federal activity against foreigners engaged in the business of prostitution. To make a case it was necessary to establish actual importation, and this was hard to do as the girls changed hands rapidly. The situation created pressure for more stringent legislation. The Bureau of Immigration almost at once prepared a bill abolishing the three-year limit on the deportation of alien anarchists, criminals, and the "sexually immoral," to be presented the next Congress.[1]

George Kibbe Turner now launched a new blast in *McClure's,* this time against the City of New York, entitled "Tammany's Control of New York by Professional Criminals." He traced the evolution of politically-organized crime on the lower East Side under Tammany leadership, notably that of "Big Tim" Sullivan and his clan of relatives, with principally Jewish and Italian subordinates. These underlings were organized largely in gangs that thrived on a variety of crime but depended most largely on prostitution for their revenue. Their members were seldom arrested, and even when picked up were let off or treated most leniently in the municipal courts because of their services to the Tammany ticket at election time. They could often decide a city-wide election, Turner declared, by repeater voting and the intimidation of the opposition. Turner quoted Police Commissioner Bingham as saying of these ganges: "We cannot get these men. If they could be caught the whole 'white slave' trade would drop, and the whole social evil be intensely ameliorated, because these men work in a regular trust." Turner noted that the local French participation in vice had declined in the last two years, and the business had been taken over largely by Jewish and Italian operators. He mentioned one particular organization, the New York Independent Benevolent Association, composed exclusively of Hebrews, which was "the society and trade organization of the Jewish dealers in prostitution."[2]

Shortly afterward Bingham was removed from office by Mayor McClellan, who was seeking to patch up his relations with Tammany, which since 1902 had been headed by Boss Charles F. Murphy. Bingham had tried hard to put the lid on gambling, vice, and other crime, not only in the Tenderloin but also in the Bowery district, in Chinatown, and on Coney Island. In the process he had incurred the wrath of the Sullivan clan, the most powerful group in Tammany Hall, and its allies in Brooklyn. His successor as police commissioner took orders meekly from the organization, and the local war on the forces of evil practically came to a halt. Judge William J. Gaynor of Brooklyn, who had attacked Bingham ferociously for what he considered his high-handed police methods and had been the occasion of his dismissal, became the Democratic candidate for mayor in the election of 1909.[3]

Toward the close of the campaign Turner sounded off again in a really sensational article in *McClure's,* entitled "The Daughters of the Poor." New York had become the world center of the White Slave Trade, he declared, surpassing even Paris and the traditional Jewish center in Lemberg. The trade was now both import and export, girls recruited largely in the tenement districts of New York being shipped all over the world, as well as to other cities throughout the United States. The traffic was largely in the hands of Jews, with Italians in second place, and both under the protection of Tammany Hall. "Shall New York continue," Turner asked rhetorically, "to be the recruiting ground for the collection for market of young women by politically organized procurers? The only practical way to stop it will be by the defeat of Tammany Hall." S. S. McClure, the publisher, accompanied this with a long editorial in the same issue, reciting the many sins of Tammany, which, he said, "has perverted civilization in New York, using the great politically untrained population for this purpose." Tammany was a threat to American civilization and must be defeated.[4]

Turner's article had a powerful but mixed effect; it became the dominant issue in the city election. The *Evening Post,* on the basis of independent investigations, confirmed his view of New York, under Tammany rule, as a great recruiting and distributing center of the White Slave traffic, which flowed heavily in both directions. "No less than three thousand girls are decoyed from Europe every year by organized bands whose headquarters are under police—hence Tammany—protection," the *Post* declared. "Twice that many victims are obtained from New York and the territory nearby." Dr. O. Edward Janney, chairman of the National Vigilance Committee, confirmed the charges that had been made in the *Post* in a lengthy telegram from Baltimore. "New York City is the chief 'white slave' market," he assured the editor. "Vigorous efforts to stamp out the evil are being made in Chicago, but they must prove largely ineffective while the evil is rampant in New York." The *Times,* speaking editorially of Turner's charges against Tammany, held that they had been confirmed from many sources. It did not matter whether Gaynor, the Democratic candidate, knew of the depth of the evil or not. "The only thing to do in the premises is to turn Tammany out." Both Boss Murphy and Judge Gaynor, naturally, denounced Turner, calling him "a hired slanderer in the columns of a muckraking and filth-throwing magazine." The real issues had been obscured "by mendacity and calumny directed against both the womanhood and manhood of the great east side" by "the selfish and unscrupulous defamers of this great city." Turner, Gaynor declared, was "a mere political and racial bigot"; he had slandered both the Jews and the Irish. The *Sun* countered this by calling Gaynor "the defender of the indefensible." "Who is there with years above sixteen and eyes opened to more than the vision of puppydom," it asked rhetorically, "who has not known that the rule political and official below Fourteenth Street has been that of a pornocracy, that the sale of the body and soul of human beings has been a part of the daily trade of the rulers of this part of the metropolis?"[5]

The controversy raged on to election day, and a strong defensive reaction developed on the East Side. Even Otto Bannard, the Republican-Fusion candidate for mayor running against Gaynor, thought that Turner had gone too far. If the conditions described actually existed, he told a *Times* reporter, he had no knowledge of them. He noticed that the magazine writer held the Jews chiefly responsible for the evil in the city which the article said existed. "I think that must be not only an error, but a serious injustice. I have always understood that both the importers and the imported are chiefly French." Louis Marshall, the distinguished Jewish leader who had been chairman of the State Immigration Commission appointed by Governor Hughes, and was supporting the Fusion ticket, was disturbed and wrote to Congressman William S. Bennet, Bannard's campaign manager, on the subject. The White Slave Trade did exist, he knew, and investigations by the Immigration Commission had shown that there were Jews involved in it, but "to hold Jews, as such, responsible for the white slave traffic throughout the world has never occurred to any right-thinking man." This crime, in all ages, he declared, "has been held in especial abhorrence by those of the Jewish faith." Lillian Wald, C. L. Sulzberger, Jacob Schiff, and other prominent Jews supporting Fusion, trying to keep the East Side in line, signed with Marshall a public statement insisting that Turner had not intended to attack any race. Bennet became afraid to circulate Turner's article as a campaign document. This did not save Bannard. There was great resentment at Turner's identification of the White Slave trade with immigrant Jews, whipped up by Tammany speakers. One influential Yiddish journal went so far as to say that it didn't matter which candidate won: "It is only important if the Jews win or their defamers." Gaynor was elected as mayor, in good part by East Side Jewish votes, though the Fusion party took most of the lesser offices and Tammany was crippled.[6]

NOTES

[1] Henry L. Stimson to Charles J. Bonaparte (Atty. Gen.), July 23, August 14, 1908, Henry L. Stimson Papers (microfilm edition), Yale University Library; "White Slave Traffic," House Report No. 47, 61st Cong., 2d Sess., Dec. 21, 1909, 6-9; Edwin W. Sims to the Immigration Commission, February 3, 1909, in *Ibid.,* 28-31; "Nations Act Against the White Slave Trade," *Charities and the Commons,* XXI (February 20, 1909), 979-980; "May the United States Prevent the Importation of Vice?" *Outlook,* XCII (May 29, 1909), 250-251; Graham Taylor, "The Police and Vice in Chicago," *Survey,* XXIII (November 6, 1909), 160-163; *Annual Report of the Commissioner-General of Immigration,* 1909, 115-116.

[2] George Kibbe Turner, "Tammany's Control of New York," 120-129.

3 *Times*, June 2, July 1, 2, 1909; "The New York Police Situation," *Outlook*, XCII (July 10, 1909), 573-575; "General Bingham's Revelations," *Ibid.* (August 28, 1909), 959-960; Theodore A. Bingham, "The New York Police in Politics," *Century Magazine*, LXXVIII (September 1909), 725-728; *Ibid.*, "The Organized Criminals of New York," *McClure's Magazine*, XXXIV (November 1909), 62-67.

4 Turner, "The Daughters of the Poor," 45-61; S. S. McClure, "The Tammanyizing of a Civilization," *McClure's Magazine*, XXXIV (November 1909), 117-128.

5 *Evening Post*, October 23, 25, 28, 1909; *Sun*, October 29, 1909; *Times*, October 24, 25, 26, 1909; "The Slave Traffic in America," *Outlook*, XCIII (November 6, 1909), 528-529.

6 *Times*, October 26, 29,30, November 3, 1909; *Post*, October 26, 1909; Arthur A. Goren, *New York Jews and the Quest for Community: The Kehillah Experiment, 1908-1922* (New York, 1970), 139-144.

X

Turner's article, and the White Slave issue that had dominated the New York City election, attracted national attention. "White slavery is a reality," the Illinois *State Register* Proclaimed, "no myth, no fiction, no dream, but a grim reality." Those who were fighting it "deserve all the encouragement, all the help and all the legislation necessary to put 'white slavery' on a par with murder. It is worse, with anything!" When Congress met in the following month, it was in the mood to pass some drastic legislation on the subject. The Immigration Commission, which had been gathering huge masses of data on the general subject of immigration since 1907, set out to give it the ammunition. The Commission's findings as a whole, in encyclopedic proportions, were not to come out for another year or so, but it now presented to Congress, through its chairman, Senator W. P. Dillingham, a preliminary report entitled "Importing Women for Immoral Purposes." This, it said, was "the most pitiful and the most revolting phase of the immigration question." As the subject was especially liable to sensational exploitation, the report was intended to be "primarily a statement of undeniable facts which may form a basis of reasonable legislation." Because of the great public interest in the subject, Senator Dillingham asked for and received permission to print 4,000 copies of the report.[1]

The Commission had found that while many innocent foreign girls were brought into the country, most of those imported were already professionals, lured by the promise of vastly improved earnings. The traffic was quite extensive, several thousands of women being imported annually. Many of them came through the Port of New York, but large numbers were now coming through Canada. The business was "strictly foreign commerce for profit." The earnings of the women might be large, but they were badly exploited by their pimps and usually by their house madams. They were often diseased, and were having a ruinous effect on American home life. Only a small proportion of the women were discovered and barred from the country, but "the greater care of the immigration officials" was producing improved results, especially at New York. There was not only importation but also extensive domestic recruiting of prostitutes, especially among ignorant foreign girls already landed in the United States. Thousands of young men, "usually those of foreign birth or the immediate sons of foreigners," were engaged in this, "the most accursed business ever devised by man," and "a disgrace to American civilization."

The principal groups importing women, the Commission had found, were French and Jewish. The French, as a rule, imported women of their own nationality. "The Jews often import or harbor Russian, Austrian, Hungarian, Polish, or German women, usually doubtless of their own race." There had been much talk of a great monopoly trafficking in women from country to country, but the Commission had been unable to learn of any such corporation and did not believe in its existence. Men engaged in the business had a large acquaintance with each other, however, and there was cooperation and some organization among them. Two organizations of importers, one French, the other Jewish, had been identified. They kept their women in brutal subjection amounting to actual slavery, at times resorting to murder to maintain discipline. Apparently they hated each other, but their members would join forces against the common enemy, the law. Both the French and the Jews in the business operated through loose associations in many cities of the United States, and there seemed also to be "a number of Italian pimps scattered throughout the country who are apparently vicious and criminal," with women of various nationalities under their control.[2]

The crusade was now at a high pitch, and debate began early in the session. But two important committees presented their separate bills and some rivalry developed. Representative Mann of Illinois, of the House Committee on Interstate and Foreign Commerce, introduced a bill to prevent the transportation of alien women in interstate as well as foreign commerce. This bill was supported by a House report closely paralleling that submitted to the Senate by the Immigration Commission. Representatives Howell of New Jersey and Bennet of New York, of the House Committee on Immigration and Naturalization, presented a measure to amend the 1907 law. It would remove the three-year limit on deportation, and revise the language of the earlier act so as to circumvent the Supreme Court decision that had vitiated it. Under the new bill, any alien "supported" by prostitution was guilty of a felony and could also be deported at the end of his term. Both bills were finally passed.[3]

The Howell-Bennet act was an immigration act and affected aliens only. Its basic feature, removing the time limit on deportation of both prostitutes and those engaged in the business as procurers, pimps, or house madams, was one that the Bureau of Immigration had been urging. Violators were made subject to up to ten years' imprisonment before deportation, though the prostitutes themselves were still subject only to deportation. Under this act the Immigration Service operated aggressively and with considerable success in the years that followed. The Mann Act, on the other hand, was a commerce act. It did not apply exclusively to aliens. In fact, the word "alien," as applied to women, had been dropped in the course of debate. The penalty for violation was five years' imprisonment, or ten years if the girl was under eighteen. The Mann Act, enforced primarily by the new Bureau of Investigation of the Department of Justice, seems to have served the purpose of cutting down sharply, though not eliminating, the interstate traffic in prostitutes. It had also some surprising side effects. As the courts upheld and came to interpret it, any young man taking a girl across a state line could be prosecuted under its terms. Many professional pimps and procurers, alien and native, were caught under it. It also brought the downfall of merely adventurous young men, and became a notorious tool of blackmail.[4]

While the Congress was passing the legislation that seems actually, over the years that followed, to have broken the back of the trade in alien prostitutes, the states and the larger cities, beginning with Chicago, were engaged in vice investigations and passing legislation designed to stamp out commercialized vice entirely. It had already been recognized that the strictly domestic business was far larger than importation, though the foreign-born were assumed to be playing the dominant role in this traffic as well. "In the United States, at least three-fourths of the girl slave victims have been inveigled from our own farms, homes, towns and cities," said Clifford Roe, who by 1910 had become a professional vice crusader, "but it was the foreigner who taught the American this dastardly business." Nativists in the crusade "envisioned well-organized networks of vice connecting European and American cities; export-import syndicates thriving on the trade of loose women, diabolical agencies forever searching for new opportunities in the American metropolis." They often embarrassed the liberal friends of aliens who were equally committed to the eradication of commercialized vice. The crusade, still building up, was adding greatly to the immigration restriction movement that brought the vastly detailed and restrictive immigration law of 1917 and the quota laws of the early 1920's. Purity organizations, such as the vigilance committees, and health crusaders , seeking to curb venereal disease joined forces. Soon the statute books were cluttered with laws and ordinances intended to break up the so-called "red-light districts" that had flourished, legally or illegally, in almost every American city. Just as the professional exhorters of the Anti-Saloon League were beginning to convince the American people that they could and should do away with alcohol, so the public had come to accept the idea that sexual vice could be stamped out.[5]

In New York City the storm of controversy roused in the last days of the electoral campaign of 1909 did not subside quickly. The Tammany organization had been badly hurt, and at least its top leadership now sought means to brighten its reputation. With considerable publicity, it called for the impanelling of a special grand jury to investigate the subject of White Slavery in the city, even though the investigation would be under a district attorney, Charles S. Whitman, who had been elected on an anti-Tammany ticket. John D. Rockefeller, Jr., was induced to become foreman. This grand jury made a much more thorough study of the question than perhaps Tammany had anticipated. It sat for nearly six months, while pimps, procurers, and prostitutes left town or made themselves as inconspicuous as possible. Whitman and his staff made extensive investigations and brought a considerable number of indictments under state law, sometimes going to the extent of buying girls from dealers in the search for evidence.

The judge, a Tammany man close to Boss Murphy, refused for some time to receive the presentment which Rockefeller wished to make, insisting that "the only point at issue was whether there existed a formal organized corporate body of men who were associated in the business of trafficking in women." The grand jury was not able to identify any organization in these terms, but it did find that "a trafficking in the bodies of women does exist and is carried on by individuals acting for their own individual benefit, and that these persons are known to each other and are more or less informally associated." It confirmed, in its presentment, the existence of the New York Independent Benevolent Association, a Jewish association of procurers stemming from the old Max Hochstim Association. This organization had figured prominently in Turner's charges and in the special report of the Immigration Commission. The grand jury did not bring an indictment against the organization, which was chartered under New York State law, but found that its members were, or had been, "engaged in the operation of disorderly houses or in living upon the proceeds of women's shame." The judge gave the press an abridged version of the presentment, which he had finally accepted, and the resulting headlines proclaimed "Rockefeller Jury Reports No White Slavery." In dismissing the jury, the judge said that their answer to the main question was "a merited rebuke to the slanderers of the cleanest great city in the world." Vice crusaders and others denounced this as a gross distortion of the jury's findings.[6]

One of the several recommendations of the Rockefeller grand jury had been that the mayor appoint a commission to make a study of the methods of dealing with the social evil in the leading cities of the United States and Europe, "with a view to devising the most effective means of minimizing the evil in this city." Mayor Gaynor was far from enthusiastic about such a commission and Rockefeller, who had become deeply interested in the problem finally decided to create a private agency on a permanent basis. He had had a forced education in an aspect of society that he had scarcely known existed. The Bureau of Social Hygiene, supported by Rockefeller money, came into existence in 1911, and for twenty-five years engaged in a broad program of studies and reforms centering around, but by no means confined to, prostitution.

NOTES

[1] "A Review of the World," *Current Literature*, XLVII(December 1909), 594-598; "Importing Women for Immoral Purposes," 3; *Congressional Record*, 61st Cong., 2d Sess., 73-74.

[2] "Importing Women for Immoral Purposes," 6-12, 23-24.

[3] *Congressional Record*, 61st Cong., 2d Sess., 8, 245, 246, 286, 517-530, 545-551, 804-823, 1031-1041, 1759-1760, 1893, 1902, 3231-3232, 3244, 3291, 3253, 3585, 3855, 8623, 9032, 9037-9040, 9117, 9118; U.S. Statutes at Large, XXXVI, Part I, No. 1, Chapter 128; *Ibid.*, No. 2, Chapter 395.

[4] Arthur C. Millspaugh, *Crime Control by the National Government* (Washington, 1937), 77-78; *Survey*, XXIX (March 8, 1913), 799-801; "White Slavers Routed," *Outlook*, CIII (March 15, 1913), 569-571; "White-Slave Law and Blackmail," *Literary Digest*, LIV (January 27, 1917), 178; Howard B. Woolston, *Prostitution in the United States* (New York, 1921), 86-87; Anthony M. Turano, "Adultery on Wheels," *American Mercury*, XXXIX (December 1936), 441-447.

[5] Clifford G. Roe, *Panders and Their White Slaves, 211-212;* Graham Taylor, "The Story of the Chicago Vice Commission," *Survey*, XXVI (May 6, 1911), 239-247; Feldman, "Prostitution, The Alien Woman and the Progressive Imagination," 194-196; Joseph Mayer, "The Passing of the Red Light District— Vice Investigations and Results," *Social Hygiene*, IV (1918), 197-209; John C. Burnham, "The Progressive Era Revolution in American Attitudes toward Sex," *The Journal of American History*, LIX (March 1973), 897-898.

6 *Herald,* January 4, 5, 1910; Theodore A. Bingham, *The Girl That Disappears: The Real Facts about the White Slave Traffic* (Boston, 1911), 19-31; "Five 'White Slave' Trade Investigations," *McClure's Magazine,* XXV (July 1910), 346-348; "The Rockefeller Grand Jury Report," *Ibid.* (August 1910), 471-473; Roe, *The Great War on White Slavery,* 217-227, 229, 232, 233; *Annual Report of the Chief Clerk of the District Attorney's Office, County of New York,* 1910, 7-9; Raymond B. Fosdick, *John D. Rockefeller, Jr., A Portrait* (New York, 1956), 137-138.

XI

In 1913, the Bureau published, as the first of a number of studies, a detailed report on commercialized prostitution in New York City, showing that vice was flourishing. There were not quite so many elegant parlor houses as there had been before the 1907 raids, but they still existed in numbers. Prostitution was also practiced openly in hotels, including some of the better ones, in houses of assignation, tenements, and massage parlors. Thanks to the work of the Committee of Fourteen, the Raines Law hotel had almost disappeared, but prostitutes were found in the back rooms of hundreds of saloons. Prostitutes and their pimps solicited openly on the streets. The business was highly commercialized, and the names and addresses of over 500 men engaged in it had been collected. "The majority are foreigners," the report said, and they often moved their operations from city to city in the United States, or to other countries as far as South America and South Africa. These were men with a substantial stake in the business. There were also probably several thousand pimps with only one or two girls working for them. Estimates of the number of prostitutes in New York ranged from 25,000 to 100,000. Nearly 15,000 of them had been counted in Manhattan alone. A large proportion of their customers were out of town visitors. The murder of the gambler, Herman Rosenthal, in the middle of July 1912, and the subsequent investigation of the Police Department, it was noted, had alarmed many of the bigger operators and a number of houses had since been closed. They were no longer sure of protection. But this was regarded as a temporary situation. There was confidence in the underworld that hard times would not last. The police "who are reputed to have worked in collusion with the exploiters of prostitutes share the same view."[1]

The author of this sensational report was George J. Kneeland, who had worked for the Committee of Fourteen and later headed the investigation for the Chicago vice commission. He was one of a number of men who had become professionals in the business. This study, the earlier one in Chicago, and similar investigations in other cities, stoked the crusading fires across the nation. Novels, plays, and moving pictures dealt with the subject of White Slavery in lurid terms. Sensationalists "developed fantasies of the underworld that thrilled and scared those who followed with difficulty the content of more serious investigations." The fear of the "White Slaver," almost always depicted as a foreigner, reached proportions of real hysteria. Stories ultimately circulated of women and girls being pricked with drugged needles in darkened movie houses or on crowded street cars, to wake up in the brothels of Buenos Aires or Constantinople.

As was probably inevitable, there was a reaction. *Current Opinion* quoted William M. Reedy, editor of the *St. Louis Mirror,* as having little use for the anti-vice crusades financed by Standard Oil money. "There are, he says, and he speaks with the authority of a man of wide experience, plenty of women of evil life in all large cities. But these are not 'White Slaves.' The inmates of houses may be in debt to mistresses, but they are not held prisoners and cannot be. But as young Rockefeller is putting up the money for the White Slave hunt, of course, . . .'White Slaves' have to be produced." Reedy thought the vice crusade business was being overdone. "There's an epidemic frenzy in it. And the public isn't so much shocked. It rather enjoys the coprolalia of it all." A little later *Current Opinion* quoted the president of the Southern Rescue Mission as confessing his failure, after six years' work among prostitutes, to discover the over-advertised "white slave." He did not believe there were a dozen girls in America in houses of ill-fame that could not walk out if they wanted to. "They love that kind of life and will scoff at the reformer and even kick him out if he does not get out when asked to." Still later *Current Opinion* quoted reputable newspapers across the country as attacking the power of the catchword "white slavery," and as attempting "to extinguish the conflagration of hysteria." But, it noted, the idea of White Slavery was "not only strongly established in the popular mind, but is one in which the public veritably revels."[2]

The Rosenthal murder, which implicated high police officials, had been followed by a detailed investigation of the Police Department conducted under Henry H. Curran, a Republican committee chairman in the Board of Aldermen. The findings of this investigation revealed extensive police protection to pimps and procurers, as well as to gamblers, gangsters, and criminals in general. Together with the concurrent prosecution of the gangsters and their police allies involved in the Rosenthal case, by District Attorney Whitman, they went far to discredit the administration of Mayor Gaynor. Gaynor had truly never been a Tammany man, and he had finally broken with the organization completely. He was planning to run as an independent in the 1913 mayoral election when he died of a heart attack. A reform Fusion ticket headed by John Purroy Mitchel swept the field.[3]

Under Mayor Mitchel and his aggressive police commissioner, Arthur Woods, gangsters, gamblers, and vice operators all had a thorough drubbing. The Committee of Fourteen, still active, gave its help. The Bureau of Social Hygiene, presenting a supplementary report on the vice situation in New York in 1915, thought that there had been great improvement. "No police commissioner has ever before grappled with the difficulty as energetically, as intelligently and as persistently as Police Commissioner Woods." The police force, as a whole, had responded to his leadership. There were few parlor houses operating, and these were quiet, open only to known customers. Operations in hotels had been reduced. Street walkers and their pimps were having a hard time. Most of the owners of disorderly houses were in hiding or had left town. "The vice ring is completely disorganized." Two years later, as the end of the Mitchel administration approached, the Bureau reported that "New York City has been made an unprofitable field of operation for these people." Many pimps had left town or gone into legitimate employment. "Madams and inmates have left for other cities, some going to Cuba, to the Panama Canal Zone, and to Alaska." Constant raiding followed by active prosecution had discouraged both male and female operators. A former vice operator was quoted as saying that his group was "scattered all over." Commissioner Woods, the *Outlook* proclaimed, had "Achieved the Impossible." He had, against all predictions, curbed the gangsters, the Black Hand, the confidence men, and commercialized vice. There were no public gambling houses of the old brazen type operating in New York; "instead of three hundred disorderly hotels there are believed to be less than twenty-five, and these are rapidly disappearing." According to one rough estimate, "instead of fifteen thousand scarlet women in Manhattan, there are only a thousand." By the time that the United States entered the first World War, New York City was probably as nearly clean of commercialized vice as it has ever been in modern times.[4]

Meanwhile the Immigration Service, using the 1910 legislation removing the time limit on deportation, had been actively and systematically combing the country for foreign prostitutes and procurers. This went on year after year, with the help of the Department of Justice and local authorities. In the spring of 1914, the *Times* reported the passage through Buffalo of two cars filled with men and women on their way to Ellis Island for deportation. "Among the forty-five women," it was learned, were "hardened residents of the underworlds of a dozen great cities, as well as many young girls from Russia, Spain, and Italy. The men represent cadets, procurers, and agents for the White Slave traffic." The train had started from San Francisco, picking up undesirables along the way. Federal marshals and Chicago detectives were in charge of the prisoners. This shipment of deportees was only one of many. In the fiscal year 1914, the Commissioner-General reported "392 immoral women, 154 procurers, 155 persons supported by the proceeds of prostitution," and a good number of criminals as having been deported. Almost as many of these classes had been debarred from entry at the ports. There had also been 44 prosecutions of importers of immoral women on evidence obtained by immigration agents, with 29 convictions. But the Commissioner General believed that this activity was only "scratching the surface," so far as the sexually immoral classes were concerned. He urged a larger appropriation to expand the work.[5]

There had been protest against the handling of women deportees, however. They, like the men, were often held in jails while awaiting the issuance of deportation warrants or transportation to Ellis Island. Their cases were routinely handled like those of criminal deportees. Mrs. Kate Waller Barrett, president of the National Council of Women and the National Florence Crittendon Missions, the Commissioner-General learned, was to attend the meeting of the International Council of Women in Rome in May. He persuaded the Department of Labor to commission Mrs. Barrett as a special agent of the Bureau of Immigration to represent it at this meeting, and at other conferences of European women on the enforcement of the White Slave treaty. Mrs. Barrett made a full report, with detailed recommendations, on her return. New regulations were accordingly drawn up by the Department providing special treatment for women deportees. In particular, they were not to be incarcerated in jails but, wherever possible, put in the custody of missionary societies of their own religion or ethnic group while awaiting disposition of their cases. There were to be women appointees at the ports of deportation in special charge of their welfare, and international arrangements were to be developed for their reception by suitable women's organizations when they were returned to their native lands.

By the time that these new humanitarian regulations were promulgated, general war had been raging in Europe for many months and deportations, in the main, had become impossible. Ellis Island began to fill up with deportees who could not be sent home. Immigration Commissioner Frederic C. Howe, municipal reformer and humanitarian, called a committee of prominent New York women, including Lillian Wald and Mary Simkhovitch, to interview the foreign girls in custody. They found that arrests had often been made on flimsy evidence, and that hearings had been brief and often without counsel or interpreters. Many of the girls were not hardened professionals and Howe, with the approval of the Secretary of Labor, paroled a good many of them until the end of the war. This action, along with others designed for the benefit of the immigrants in detention but cutting the profits of commercial interests, made enemies for him and contributed to his forced resignation later. His refusal to deport radicals without a hearing during the big Red Scare of 1919-1920 was, however, its precipitating cause.[6]

After the end of the war the program of deportation was resumed. The reduction of immigration to a comparative trickle during the war, and the imposition of the quota laws shortly afterward, no doubt reduced the incoming vice traffic materially. Nevertheless, the field agents of the Bureau of Immigration continued to pick up a good many foreign prostitutes, procurers, and vice operators for deportation, and almost as many such types were stopped at the gates. The Commissioner-General of Immigration reported for the fiscal year 1924 that of the 6,409 aliens deported, 339 were "prostitutes, procurers, and other immoral classes." Of the 30,284 rejected at the ports of entry, 313 were listed as in these categories. The Mann Act, enforced by what was now known as the Federal Bureau of Investigation, continued to function, slowing interstate traffic in alien as well as native American girls. But the crusading fever in this field, as in other reforms of the pre-war era, had abated. There was little talk of White Slavery as a problem. There were those optimists who believed that the imposition of national Prohibition in 1920, by banishing the saloon, had materially reduced prostitution in general. This appears doubtful. Prohibition itself had corrupted local law enforcement agencies appallingly, and police officers on the take from bootleggers were little likely to refuse protection money from vice operators. Nevertheless, in New York and other cities, open display of prostitution had unquestionably been cut down. The proportion of aliens engaged in the business seems to have been greatly reduced.

NOTES

[1] Graham Taylor, "The War on Vice," *Survey*, XXIX (March 8, 1913), 811; "Rockefeller Report on Commercialized Vice," *Ibid.*, XXX(May 24, 1913), 257-259; Committee of Fifteen, *The Social Evil* (1912 ed.), 212-214; Fosdick, *Rockefeller*, 138-140; George J. Kneeland, *Commercialized Prostitution in New York City* (New York, 1913), 3-162.

[2] Filler, *Crusaders for American Liberalism*, 292-293; Henry F. May, *The End of American Innocence* (New York, 1959),343-344; Lubove, "The Progres-

sives and the Prostitute," 315-316; *Current Opinion,* LV (August 1913), 113-114; *Ibid.* (November 1913), 348; *Ibid.,* LVI (February 1914), 129.

3 Henry H. Curran, *Pillar to Post* (New York, 1941), 151-174; Edwin R. Lewinson, *John Purroy Mitchel, the Boy Mayor of New York* (New York, 1965), 86-87, 95; Werner, *Tammany Hall,* 402, 522-528, 556-557; *Times,* September 12, November 5, 1913.

4 "Gaining Control Over Vice in New York," *Survey,* XXIII (February 27, 1915), 572; "The Wreck of Commercialized Vice," *Ibid.,* XXV (February 5, 1916), 532-533; Frank M. White, "A Man Who has Achieved the Impossible," *Outlook,* CXVII(September 26, 1917), 124-126; Bureau of Social Hygiene, *Commercialized Prostitution in New York City, November 1, 1915. A Comparison between 1912 and 1915* (New York, 1916), Introduction, 4-5, 12-13; *Ibid.,* November 1, 1917 (New York, 1918), 16-18.

5 *Times,* April 10, 1914; *Annual Report of the Commissioner-General of Immigration,* 1914, 7-8. .

6 *Ibid.,* 14-16, 359-386; Commissioner-General of Immigration Caminetti to Mrs. Kate Waller Barrett, April 15, 1914, File 53,678/155, General Immigration Records, Record Group 85, National Archives; Mrs. Barrett to Caminetti, May 9, 27, 1914, *Ibid.*; Amendment of Rule 22 of Immigration Rules, Adding thereto Provisions for Special Procedure in Cases of Arrested Women and Girls, Office of the Secretary, Department of Labor, April 6, 1915, *Ibid.*; Howe Commissioner-General, February 4, 1915 19/31, Labor Department Records, Record Group 174, National Archives; Frederic C. Howe, *The Confessions of a Reformer* (New York, 1925), 266-272, 273-276, 326-328.

XII

The White Slave traffic, in the original and narrow sense of an international trade in young girls, ceased to be a serious problem as far as the United States was concerned. Recruiting for the profession was overwhelmingly domestic. But meanwhile, prevailing poverty in war-stricken Europe, together with the loss of manpower during the war, provided ample material for such a traffic, and there were other markets for it. The League of Nations became concerned about it and conducted a three-year, world-wide investigation with money and experts supplied by the Rockefellers. Its report, published late in 1927, found the traffic still flourishing in many lands, but gave the United States a relatively clean bill of health. Except for some continued smuggling of Chinese girls to the Pacific Coast, "the United States was found to be hard to enter, and still harder to use as a base of operations." Many of the chief operators in New York City, the League reported, had gone into the bootlegging business or even into "something respectable."[1]

A few years later, when special prosecutor Thomas E. Dewey broke up the vice syndicate that gangster Lucky Luciano had created in New York, to take up the slack in bootlegging produced by the repeal of Prohibition, there was no suggestion that he had to import his girls. Insofar as they were not recruited locally, they came from the country and the factory towns of Pennsylvania, Ohio, Indiana, and other states. J. Edgar Hoover, chief of the Federal Bureau of Investigation, not to be outdone, promptly announced with some fanfare an aggressive campaign against White Slavery. Its most dramatic achievement seems to have been the arrest of Mae Scheible, the "New York Vice Queen," on Mann Act charges. She had transported five young women from Pittsburgh to New York. The "oldest profession in the world" still flourished in New York and elsewhere in the United States, but it seems to have been (and still to be) pretty much an intramural business.[2]

NOTES

[1] *Annual Report to the Commissioner-General of Immigration,* 1924, 10, 12; Frederick H. Whitin, "Cleaning Up New York," *National Municipal Review,* XII (November 1923), 655-662; "Fighting the World Traffic in Women and Children," *American Review of Reviews,* LXIX (January 1924), 102; Dame Edith Lyttleton, "The League's Big Little Jobs," *Outlook,* CXXXVIII (November 19, 1924), 448-450; "The Nations' Infamy," *Literary Digest,* XCIII (May 14, 1927), 32; "Trade Routes of White Slavers," *Survey,* LIX (January 15, 1928), 486-488; Willoughby C. Waterman, *Prostitution and Its Repression in New York City, 1900-1931* (New York, 1932), 46-48.

[2] Craig Thompson and Allen Raymond, *Gang Rule in New York: The Story of a Lawless Era* (New York, 1940), 389-391; James Benet, "New York's Vice Ring," *New Republic,* LXXXVII (June 10, 1936), 124-126: " 'G Men' Cen-

ter Upon White Slavers," *Literary Digest,* CXXII (August 29, 1936), 26-28; Forest Davis, "The Biggest Racketeer Falls," *Saturday Evening Post,* CCX (October 30, 1937), 12-13, 65, 67, 70-72.

IMPORTATION
AND
HARBORING
OF
WOMEN
FOR
IMMORAL
PURPOSES

61ST CONGRESS }
2d Session }

SENATE

{ DOCUMENT
{ No. 196

IMPORTING WOMEN FOR IMMORAL PURPOSES

A PARTIAL REPORT FROM THE IMMIGRATION COMMISSION ON THE IMPORTATION AND HARBORING OF WOMEN FOR IMMORAL PURPOSES

PRESENTED BY MR. DILLINGHAM

DECEMBER 10, 1909.—Referred to Committee on Immigration and ordered to be printed.

WASHINGTON
GOVERNMENT PRINTING OFFICE
1909

THE IMMIGRATION COMMISSION,
Washington, D. C., December 10, 1909.
To the Sixty-first Congress:

I have the honor to transmit herewith, on behalf of the Immigration Commission, a partial report to Congress on the Importation and Harboring of Women for Immoral Purposes.

Respectfully,

W. P. DILLINGHAM,
Chairman.

TABLE OF CONTENTS.

IMPORTATION AND HARBORING OF WOMEN FOR IMMORAL PURPOSES.

I.

INTRODUCTION.

The importation and harboring of alien women and girls for immoral purposes and the practice of prostitution by them—the so-called "white-slave traffic"—is the most pitiful and the most revolting phase of the immigration question. It is in violation of the immigration law and of the treaty made with leading European powers.[a] This business has assumed large proportions and it has been exerting so evil an influence upon our country that the Immigration Commission felt compelled to make it the subject of a thorough investigation. Since the subject is especially liable to sensational exploitation, it is important that the report be primarily a statement of undeniable facts which may form a basis of reasonable legislative and administrative action to lessen its evils.

METHODS OF INVESTIGATION.

The investigation was begun in November, 1907, under the active supervision of a special committee of the Immigration Commission; the work was conducted by a special agent in charge, with numerous assistants. Too much credit can not be given to the agents who independently planned details and with cheerful courage, even at the risk of their lives at times, secured the information. Several of the agents under various pretexts had to associate on friendly terms with the criminal procurers,[b] importers,[c] and pimps[d] and their unfortunate or degraded victims when a discovery of their purposes might have resulted in their murder. One woman agent was attacked and beaten, escaping serious injury, if not murder, only with the greatest difficulty, and yet the next day she went cheerfully back to her work, though of course in another locality, where she was not known. Special information has been secured from men who had themselves acted as keepers of disorderly houses, from women who were managing them, from physicians who had practiced in them, from women who had formerly been prostitutes, and

---

[a] See Appendixes I-A and I-B for the law and treaty covering this subject.

[b] Procurer: A man or woman who induces another, by whatever means, to enter a house of prostitution or to subject herself to another in prostitution.

[c] Importer: A man or woman who brings another into the country. He may be the procurer, or the keeper of a house, who has already arranged for her coming, but needs an agent to assist in entering the country.

[d] Pimp: A man who wholly or in part lives upon the earnings of a girl or woman who practices prostitution. Usually he is supposed to give some protection and care in return.

from those who had been brought into the country for immoral purposes under false pretenses. These persons sometimes still continued their friendly relations with those engaged in prostitution and the importation of women, although they themselves have abandoned the life. Credit should also be given to the police, court officials, and business men whose circumstances were such that their cooperation was especially helpful.[a]

The investigation has covered the cities of New York, Chicago, San Francisco, Seattle, Portland, Salt Lake City, Ogden, Butte, Denver, Buffalo, Boston, and New Orleans. In some of these cities months have been given to making a thorough investigation; in others, only time enough to gain a general knowledge of conditions. The work has also been supplemented at times by arrests and prosecution in the courts.

In order to insure accuracy, care was first taken in the selection of agents and witnesses, but, beyond that, statements have invariably been checked by placing the work of one agent against that of another, by testing the reports through arrests and trials, and by documentary material. In certain cases, naturally, the commission has relied upon the statements of the agents and others, based upon their personal observations and knowledge.

No attempt has been made to investigate conditions in every important city. Enough evidence has been secured from localities sufficiently scattered with reference to women of different races and nationalities and living under different conditions to warrant the belief that further investigation as a basis for legislative and administrative action is not needed.

SOME TANGIBLE RESULTS.

It has been a source of satisfaction to the commission to know that while the purpose of the investigation has been primarily to secure a knowledge of conditions on which to base legislation, nevertheless it has been possible so to use these facts that justice could be meted out to some of these nefarious offenders and that results have been secured of substantial value in correcting evil conditions which had been discovered.' In many instances when information had been secured regarding these criminal acts, it was necessary to delay the presentation of the facts to the prosecuting officers in order to prevent the discovery of the commission's agents by the criminals, thus checking the progress of the investigation. Later, however, both to test the reliability of the evidence secured and to bring offenders to justice as soon as it could properly be done, the evidence was laid before the proper officials in order that they might institute proceedings. In the city of New York one of the most unscrupulous and successful

---

[a] The agent in general charge of the field work of the investigation had previously had much experience as a probation officer and prosecutor of persons engaged in keeping disorderly houses. This agent's assistant also did excellent work in independent investigation and in preparation of the report. Several of the other investigators deserve the thanks of the commission and the public for their efficiency, but owing to the confidential nature of their work it is unwise to mention their names.

The cooperation of General Bingham, commissioner of police in New York City, and Mr. Arthur Woods, fourth deputy commissioner, in charge of the detective force, was particularly helpful in the East, while in Chicago the cooperation of Mr. Sims, the United States district attorney, and his assistants was absolutely essential to the success of the work.

importers and harborers, as the result of information supplied by the commission, plead guilty and was sentenced to prison, while several other cases were prosecuted by the district attorney which resulted in the breaking up of the houses and the discontinuance of the business, even though in two or three instances; in spite of favorable charges by the presiding judge, conviction was not secured on account of disagreement of the jury.

In Seattle a score or more of arrests were made and prosecutions instituted with which the commission's agents had a more or less close connection, while in Chicago the United States district attorney goes so far as to give credit to the agents of the commission for the remarkable success of numerous prosecutions instituted by him on their information. In a letter, printed in full in the note,[a] to a member of the commission under date of February 3, 1909, he says:

Information and data furnished us and the assistance given to us by the special agents of the commission were invaluable. The cooperation of the commission made possible the institution and successful prosecution of many of the cases brought in this district. I have always felt that without the aid which the commission was able to give it would not have been possible for us to have accomplished what has been done.

---

[a] DEPARTMENT OF JUSTICE,
OFFICE OF UNITED STATES ATTORNEY, NORTHERN DISTRICT OF ILLINOIS,
826–833 Federal Building, Chicago, February 3, 1909.

In compliance with the suggestion that I furnish you with a statement of the work done by the United States attorney's office at Chicago, in connection with the prosecution of violations of section 3 of the act of July 1, 1907—the so-called "white-slave law"—I have the honor to state:

Reports of numerous violations of this law were first made to this office early in 1908 by slum workers and the members of charitable and humane organizations which labor in the red-light districts. As a result of preliminary investigations which I caused to be made, I reached the conclusion that the law was being violated on an extensive scale. Accordingly, in May, warrants were sworn out for the arrest of eight or ten keepers, charging them with the detention of alien girls. Notwithstanding the fact that this office exercised every precaution to keep the proposed arrests secret, the matter in some way leaked out, and when the deputy United States marshals went to the Twenty-second street district to make the arrests, all of the parties wanted had mysteriously disappeared. After making some ineffectual attempts to locate these parties, I reached the conclusion that without some specially trained force it would be practically impossible, with the regular force of the office, to secure successful results.

It was at this stage of the proceedings that you called at the office and advised me that you were in a position to turn over to me information which had been collected by the agents of the Immigration Commission, and also that the agents of the commission, who were at that time collecting data and information in this district, would turn the same over to us to aid us in the prosecutions. I found that the information which had been collected by the agents of the commission was exactly what we wanted, and acting on it a few days later we made several raids, which resulted in a large number of arrests. Since that time, largely as a result of the information which has been furnished us by the agents of the commission, we have made other arrests and have prosecuted a number of cases to a successful conclusion.

From what I know of the situation I am convinced that the prosecutions have had a most salutary effect, at least in this district. Of a large number of persons who a few months ago were actively engaged in the importation of alien women and girls for immoral purposes, some are serving sentences of imprisonment, others have forfeited bail and fled, and reliable information which comes to me is to the effect that no inconsiderable number have become so frightened at the prosecutions that they have abandoned their practices, left the city, and gone into other business.

It is also clear that the prosecutions have resulted in greatly reducing the number of alien women harbored in the establishments in the Chicago red-light districts. Information in my possession is to the effect that a considerable number of them have returned to the country whence they came, while others have gone to other States in the United States.

An interesting fact in this connection is that in one case alone the district attorney collected in forfeited bail and fines enough money to pay twice over the cost of the commission's entire investigation of the subject.

THE REASONS FOR THE BUSINESS.

To the motive of business profit is due beyond question the impulse which creates and upholds this traffic. The procurers who seduce or otherwise entice the women to leave their foreign homes, the importers who assist them in evading the law or who bring them into the United States for sale, the pimps and keepers of disorderly houses who exploit them body and soul, have only profit in view. The work is strictly foreign commerce for profit.

Although very many of the girls are brought here innocent, betrayed into a slavery rigid in its strictness and barbarous in its nature, the prize offered to the victim is only that of higher wages and better economic conditions. The much greater number of

---

I think I may safely say that the prosecutions we have conducted have resulted in effectually breaking up the traffic in alien girls, at least in this district and for the time being. I have been informed by those who are in position to know that as the result of the prosecutions instituted the value of the establishments in the Chicago red-light districts have depreciated 50 per cent. In addition to a number of establishments which have been closed a considerable number have changed hands. These transfers show that the consideration was much less than the going price of such concerns one year ago.

In this connection I want to express to you my appreciation of the assistance which has been furnished by the Immigration Commission. The information and data furnished us and the assistance given to us by the special agents of the commission were invaluable. The cooperation of the commission made possible the institution and successful prosecution of many of the cases brought in this district. I have always felt that without the aid which the commission was able to give us it would have been impossible for us to have accomplished what has been done.

The cases instituted in this district and the results to date in each case are as follows:

Alphonse and Eva Dufaur; six indictments for harboring six alien women; bail fixed at $25,000; bail forfeited; defendants supposed to have fled to France; place of business in this city abandoned. Our information is to the effect that owing to sacrifices in the disposition of their property, made necessary by their hurried departure, the Defaurs were put to an expense, including the forfeited bail, of about $80,000. The Dufaurs are supposed to have been among the leading French importers in the United States.

August Duval and Marie Duval were the proprietors of a French restaurant and hotel which was supposed to have been used as a rendezvous for French importers and alien women brought to this country; fined $1,000 and $100 and costs, respectively, on plea of guilty to conspiracy. They have closed up their hotel, disposed of their property, and, I am advised, have returned to France.

Fernand Bocquet, indicted for harboring with the Dufaurs and Duvals; fined $100 and costs.

Henry Lair, indicted for importation and harboring; found guilty on a plea of nolo contendere; sentenced to two years in the penitentiary at Fort Leavenworth and to pay a fine of $2,500. The testimony in the Lair case showed that, in addition to having an agent permanently stationed in Paris, he, each year, sent agents abroad for the purpose of procuring girls. He had establishments in Chicago and San Francisco, making his headquarters at the latter place. The girls who were imported as a result of his activities were distributed at various points in the United States from New York and San Francisco.

Lucienne D'Arville (Mrs. Harry Lair), indicted as an accomplice of Lair; fined $100 on plea of guilty.

Joseph Oschner, indicted for harboring German girl; tried, convicted, and sentenced to two and a half years in the Leavenworth Penitentiary and to pay a fine of $2,500.

Joseph Keller, indicted for harboring Hungarian girls; tried, convicted, and sentenced to eighteen months at Fort Leavenworth Penitentiary and to pay costs.

women who have already been living an immoral life abroad and who come to the United States willingly to continue open-eyed the practices of their former life, come to secure higher wages, often profits ten times as great as those they have received in Europe. Even though they are subject to their pimps and have little or no opportunity to save for themselves, there is yet the opportunity for higher gains, a higher economic standard of living, an opportunity for travel, and the interest of a new environment, and perhaps at times a hope of a real betterment of conditions. But the persons chiefly responsible for the development of the traffic are not the women themselves, but the keepers of houses, the pimps, and procurers who live by their exploitation.

EXTENT OF THE TRAFFIC.

The nature of the business precludes, of course, exact statistics regarding the extent of the traffic as to the number of women imported

---

Louis Ullman, indicted for harboring Hungarian girls; tried, convicted, and sentenced to eighteen months at Fort Leavenworth Penitentiary and to pay costs.

B. H. Markel, alias Barney Markel, in business with Keller and Ullman; evaded arrest and fled. We are advised that he is now in South Africa. The proceedings against Keller, Ullman, and Markel resulted in the closing up of two establishments in the South Chicago districts.

Joseph Bolar, indicted for harboring Hungarian girls; sentenced to thirty days in the house of correction on a plea of guilty. As a result of Bolar's conviction, the place previously operated by him at South Chicago has been closed. Others who were in business with Bolar evaded arrest and fled.

Sol Rubin, indicted for harboring Canadian girl; tried, convicted, and sentenced to nine months in the house of correction and fined $25.

Louis Rosenblum, indicted with Rubin for harboring Canadian girl; fined $400 and sentenced to the house of correction for one day on a plea of guilty.

Matilda Stern, indicted for harboring a French-Canadian girl; tried, convicted, and sentenced to sixty days in the house of correction and to pay a fine of $250.

Joseph Michel, alias "Michel, the Mysterious;" sentenced to two weeks in the house of correction and fined $2,000 and costs on a plea of guilty to an indictment charging him with harboring French girls. The establishment operated by Michel and his wife was closed up and Michel has gone east and entered legitimate business.

Mariette Michel, indicted in connection with Joseph Michel; sentenced to two days in the house of correction and fined $500 on a plea of guilty.

Andrew Wiborg, tried and convicted for harboring a Danish girl; sentenced to forty-one days in the Cook County jail. The establishment operated by him closed as the result of his conviction.

Barney Rubin, fined $200 on a plea of guilty charging him with harboring Hungarian girl.

Morris Rothstein, fined $200 on a plea of guilty charging him with harboring Hungarian girls.

Rosie Baum, sentenced to ten days in the Cook County jail on a plea of guilty to indictment charging her with harboring Hungarian girl. The establishment operated by her was closed as the result of her conviction.

Isaac Cooperman, tried and convicted of harboring a Canadian girl. Served six months in the county jail.

Isaac Aronson, sentenced to sixty days in the house of correction on a plea of guilty.

Rosie Markel, sentenced to one week in the house of correction and fined $200 and costs on plea of guilty.

Victor Malezan, indicted for harboring Bohemian girl; case not yet tried.

There are also pending in the district three indictments against parties for harboring, who have evaded service.

At the time of the imposition of most of the sentences shown above, the court took into consideration the fact that in many instances the defendant had already spent five or six months in jail in default of bail.

Very truly, yours,   EDWIN W. SIMS,
United States Attorney.

or the number of importers. The investigation covered only those known as public prostitutes, not those practicing prostitution clandestinely. In the judgment of practically everyone who has had an opportunity for careful judgment, the numbers imported run well into the thousands each year.

For the purpose of guiding legislation, however, of more importance than statistical numbering is the collection of information regarding individual cases which show the methods of recruiting women for importation, the skill employed in evading detection by officers of the law, the measures used in exploiting to the utmost the beauty and charm of the victims and the results of the traffic upon the women themselves and upon the community. Enough individual cases have been examined to form a basis for accurate judgment.

RECRUITING.

The recruiting of alien women or girls to enter the United States in violation of section 3 of the immigration act, or to live in this country in violation of this provision of law, is carried on both here and abroad. The procurers, with cunning knowledge of human nature, play upon the weaknesses of vanity and pride, upon the laudable thrift and desire to secure a better livelihood, upon the praiseworthy trust and loyalty which innocent girls have for those to whom they have given their affection, even upon their sentiments of religion, to get their victims into their toils; and then in the pursuit of their purposes, with a cruelty at times fiendish in its calculating coldness and brutality, they exploit their attractions to the uttermost. If the woman is young and affectionate, as often happens, the procurer makes her acquaintance, treats her kindly, offers to assist her in securing a better livelihood. Her confidence and affection won, she is within his power, and is calculatingly led into a life of shame. If the procurer is a woman, the innocent girl is usually promised pleasant work for large pay.

In a large majority of cases, probably, the women imported contrary to the provisions of our law have already been leading an immoral life and are brought to this country to continue the life begun abroad. In many instances they believe that they can greatly improve their conditions, even though they recognize the power of the procurer.

IMPORTATION.

To secure entries into the country contrary to our law, these immoral women or the deluded innocent victims of the procurers are usually brought in as wives or near relatives of their importers. If they come with women, they are represented as either their maids or relatives. In the case of the Japanese, they often come to join a man to whom, in accordance with the customs of their country, they have been married by proxy. Many of these women come through the port of New York. Of late, many come by way of Canada. On the Pacific coast, San Francisco and Seattle are the chief ports of entry.

Generally these women come second class so as, first, to avoid the expense of first-class passage; second, to escape detection, as they would presumably be noticed as out of place in the first cabin. Care is usually taken to have them booked to some pretended relative or friend, or to some person, presumably respectable, although in many instances, as will be seen, an examination of steamship manifests shows that sometimes they have been booked to disreputable places.

To escape the penalty of deportation, the confirmed alien prostitute is sometimes ready to marry an American citizen or often a pimp or procurer, and thus by procuring citizenship secure admittance and retain residence in the country. The detection of these frauds is extremely difficult.

Moreover, the immigration authorities are often at a loss to know how to settle the problem with wisdom and patriotism. Shall the immigration authorities debar from landing a young woman with child by an American citizen or a domiciled alien who is willing to marry her? Shall such a woman be debarred and returned to a life of shame when, if admitted, she may well look forward to a life of content and usefulness? Many foreigners would not consider her condition disgraceful if she marries the father of her child.

SYSTEM OF EXPLOITATION.

Most pitiful for the women, and most brutal on the part of the men, are the methods employed for exploiting these women imported contrary to law, both those coming willingly to lead a vicious life and those lured into the country as innocent girls by deception and by their affections.

With rare exceptions not only the innocent women imported into this country, but the prostitutes as well, are associated with men whose business it is to protect them, direct them, and control them, and who frequently, if not usually, make it their business to plunder them unmercifully. A rigid administration of the law, driving girls out of disorderly houses, depriving them of their earnings on the streets, seems at times to drive the girls for protection and care into the clutches of the pimps, who as the price of their care take most or all their earnings; and now this system of subjection to a man has become common. The procurer or the pimp may put his woman into a disorderly house, sharing profits with the madam. He may sell her outright; he may act as an agent for another man; he may keep her, making arrangements for her hunting men. She must walk the streets and secure her patrons, to be exploited, not for her own sake but for that of her owner. Often he does not tell her even his real name. She knows his haunts, where she may send him word in case of arrest. She knows the place given her to which she must come every night and give him all her earnings. She must deny her importation, must lie regarding her residence, her address, and the time she has been in the country. If she tries to leave her man, she is threatened with arrest. If she resists, she finds all the men about her leagued against her; she may be beaten; in some cases when she has betrayed her betrayer she has been murdered.

When placed in a house she is sometimes kindly treated by her man and the madam under whom she works, provided she is submissive and attractive and profitable.

Her earnings may be large—ten times as much in this country as in eastern Europe. She may at times earn in one day from two to four times as much as her washerwoman can earn in a week, but of these earnings she generally gets practically nothing; if she is docile

57

and beautiful and makes herself a favorite with the madam, she may occasionally be allowed to ride in the parks handsomely dressed; she may wear jewelry to attract a customer; but of her earnings the madam will take one-half; she must pay twice as much for board as she would pay elsewhere; she pays three or four times the regular price for clothes that are furnished her; and when these tolls have been taken by the madam, little or nothing is left. She is usually kept heavily in debt in order that she may not escape; and besides that, her exploiters keep the books and often cheat her out of her rightful dues, even under the system of extortion which she recognizes.

Frequently she is not allowed to leave the house except in company with those who will watch her; she is deprived of all street clothing; she is forced to receive any visitor who chooses her to gratify his desires, however vile or unnatural; she often contracts loathsome and dangerous diseases and lives hopelessly on, looking forward to an early death.

RESULTS.

This importation of women for immoral purposes has brought into the country evils even worse than those of prostitution. In many instances the professionals who come have been practically driven from their lives of shame in Europe on account of their loathsome diseases; the conditions of vice obtaining there have even lowered the standard of degradation of prostitution formerly customary here. Unnatural practices are brought largely from Continental Europe, and the ease and apparent certainty of profit has led thousands of our younger men, usually those of foreign birth or the immediate sons of foreigners, to abandon the useful arts of life to undertake the most accursed business ever devised by man.

This traffic has intensified all the evils of prostitution which, perhaps more than any other cause, through the infection of innocent wives and children by dissipated husbands and through the mental anguish and moral indignation aroused by marital unfaithfulness, has done more to ruin homes than any other single cause.

This statement of the conditions found by the agents of the commission may seem strong. The more detailed statements of the facts, with evidence upon which they are made, will show that the picture is not painted in too dark colors and will make evident the necessity of remedial legislation to check the traffic, which, perhaps more than any other one thing, is a disgrace to American civilization.

II.

EXTENT OF TRAFFIC.

As was intimated in the introductory chapter, it is obviously impossible to secure figures showing the exact extent of the exploitation of women and girls in violation of the immigration act.

The annual reports of the Commissioner-General of Immigration give some indication of the extent of this illegal importation, although of course only a small percentage of those arriving in this country are discovered and debarred at the port of entry or afterwards apprehended and deported. His reports, however, show that during the past five fiscal years, 1904 to 1908, 205 alien women were prevented from entering the United States on the ground that they were prostitutes; 9 of these women were debarred in 1904, 24 in 1905, 30 in 1906, 18 in 1907, 124 in 1908.

During the same five years 49 persons were debarred because of their connection with the business of importing women for immoral purposes; 3 were debarred in 1904, 4 in 1905, 2 in 1906, 1 in 1907, 43 in 1908. The great increase in the number of those rejected in 1908 is doubtless due to the more stringent provisions of the new law of February 20, 1907, and particularly to the greater care of the immigration officials.

According to the reports of the Bureau of Immigration, during the fiscal year ending June 30, 1908, 130 aliens were deported because of violations of section 3 of the immigration act. These figures indicate that the number of cases deported is greater than the number debarred. It is, of course, easier to secure evidence of women actually engaged in prostitution within a period of three years from the date of their entry than to determine at the time of their arrival that they are imported for such purposes.

In 1909 a more rigorous policy was adopted by the bureau. Under an order of March 18, 1908, immigration officials, especially selected because of their qualifications, were assigned specifically to this work in different sections of the country, with instructions to canvass actively their respective districts for aliens subject to arrest and deportation for this cause. Naturally it would take these officials some time to get into touch with the situation, but even so, the results were very noticeable. The following table shows the number of arrests and deportations from January 1 to July 1, 1909. The increase in May and June over the preceding months is very striking and gratifying.

Arrests and deportations.

	Arrests.	Deportations.
1909.		
January	73	a 32
February	73	a 32
March	75	a 33
April	80	33
May	133	41
June	103	102

aAverage.

Of course, the number of deportations is much smaller than that of the arrests, because the effectiveness of the law, so far as deportations are concerned, has been very greatly lessened by the decision of the United States Supreme Court in the Keller case,[a] in which the court declared unconstitutional that portion of the law under which persons were prosecuted for "harboring" alien women for immoral purposes. Naturally it is much more difficult to weave a chain of evidence about an importer or procurer than to convict a person of "harboring." In consequence, convictions are not so frequent.

The records of the Bureau of Immigration show that more prostitutes and procurers are arrested and deported from the port of New

a213 U. S. Supreme Court, 138.

York than from any other port. Next in importance comes Montreal, Canada, representing the port of entry of Quebec, and then, in order, Seattle, Wash., San Francisco, Cal., San Antonio, Tex., Boston, Cleveland, Chicago, and so on.

The reports of the Commissioner of Immigration do not show the nationality or race of either the prostitute or the procurer debarred or deported under the law.

NATIONALITY.

The records of Ellis Island, the most important port, show during the period from January 1, 1907, to December 31, 1908, the following results:

Nationality.	Prostitutes at time of entry.	Began prostitution after entry.	Total.
French	15	31	46
Hebrews	1	12	13
Germans	7	6	13
Italians	4	6	10
	27	55	82

Not more than 3 women of any other nationality of a total of 93 were deported during that period.

During the period from November 15, 1908, to March 15, 1909, an agent of the Immigration Commission examined all alien women convicted in the night court of the city of New York of soliciting on the streets and of being inmates of disorderly houses. Out of the total number convicted, 48 out of 61 who had been in the country four years or less, acording to the data secured by this agent, were liable to deportation under the provisions of section 3. Table I shows the number of convictions by general nativity and race during the period from November 15, 1908, to March 15, 1909.

TABLE I.—*Disorderly house and soliciting cases in the night court of New York from November 15, 1908, to March 15, 1909.*

[This table includes those fined, held, sent to workhouse, or reprimanded.]

General nativity and race.	Number.	General nativity and race.	Number.
Native born	1,512	Foreign born—Continued.	
		Magyar	9
Foreign born:		Mexican	3
African, negro	1	Polish	10
Canadian, French	1	Scandinavian	9
Croatian	1	Scotch	4
Danish	2	Slovak	1
Dutch	2	Spanish	3
English	19	Swedish	1
Finnish	1		
Flemish	6	Total foreign born	581
French	154		
German	69	Grand total	2,093
Hebrew	225		
Irish	29		
Italian—			
North	5		
South	26		

The record was kept carefully for the last month of this period, so as to be sure that the same person was not counted more than once, even though she may have been arrested and convicted several times. This table shows the number of those convicted during this month by general nativity and race, and as indicated shows the number of different persons.

TABLE II.—*Disorderly house and soliciting cases in the night court of New York from February 16 to March 15, 1909.*

[This table includes those fined, held, sent to workhouse, and reprimanded.]

General nativity and race.	Number.	General nativity and race.	Number.
Native born..........................	166	Foreign born—Continued.	
		Magyar........................	4
Foreign born:		Polish.........................	2
Danish.........................	1	Scotch.........................	1
Dutch..........................	1	Spanish........................	1
English.........................	4	Swedish........................	1
French..........................	13		
German.........................	8	Total foreign born..............	74
Hebrew.........................	23		
Irish...........................	9	Grand total...................	240
Italian, south	6		

Appendix II gives the date of the last arrival in the United States of foreign-born persons convicted in the night court of New York of practicing prostitution in disorderly houses and of soliciting, from November 15, 1908, to March 15, 1909. This includes those fined, held, sent to workhouse, or reprimanded. It will be noted that very few of those convicted acknowledge that they have arrived in this country within a period of three years. Such acknowledgment would of course subject them to deportation. Most of them apparently find it safer to name a period of from five to ten years. The figures are not to be looked upon as exact, but rather as indicating the knowledge of the law and of means adopted to evade it.

As already intimated, these figures clearly represent but a small percentage of the number of persons engaged in violating the law. This would be presumed by anyone at all familiar with the conditions, and from the nature of the business itself. The police and the social workers in the various cities all agree with this opinion.

The figures do indicate probably somewhat the nationality and race of those engaged in the business, as shown by the records of the night court of the city of New York. Tables 1 and 2 give a fairly accurate indication of natives and aliens, showing the number of convictions. In that way they may be some indication of the relative numbers of the nationalities and races of persons practicing prostitution on the streets of New York City; but even in that respect they are liable to be misleading, inasmuch as the number of persons brought to the court-house would doubtless depend somewhat upon the section of the city in which the arrests were made, and somewhat upon the skill of the persons concerned in evading arrest or in dealing with the police.

No indication is found in any of the tables as to whether the women convicted began the practice of prostitution after they had arrived in this country or whether they were already professional street walkers before arrival. If, instead of judging by the statistics, we

61

were to take the opinions of our agents, secured by talking with the women, with the police, and with others familiar with the situation, it seems probable that the percentage of French women who practiced prostitution before arrival in this country, as compared with their total number, is decidedly larger than the percentage of Hebrews who have engaged in that business before coming. Apparently the activity of the Jewish procurers and pimps in seducing young girls to turn them into this life in this country is greater than that of the French, whereas the French are somewhat more willing to adopt the bolder and perhaps on the whole more profitable plan of importing women who are already familiar with the life.

III.

RECRUITING.

RECRUITING OF IMMORAL WOMEN.

Of far greater significance than the fact that the national law concerning the importation of alien women and girls has been violated are the facts showing the methods employed and the inadequacy of the law itself to protect our country against such importation. But even before a consideration of the specific methods of evading the law, or a discussion of the system used in the exploitation of these women, it is important to understand the way in which they are recruited to enter the country or to live here in violation of law.

In this connection, also, it is obviously impossible to give statistics showing whether the greater number are recruited abroad, or whether they are induced or compelled to enter the business after their arrival in the United States. In either case the methods of recruiting do not differ materially. Though in all probability many are innocent, the majority of women and girls who are induced to enter this country for immoral purposes have already entered the life at home and come to this country as they would go elsewhere, influenced primarily by business considerations. They believe they can make higher profits here. According to reports made by Marcus Braun, a special agent of the Bureau of Immigration, who investigated in Europe the exportation of women to America for immoral purposes, there is a practical certainty of greatly increased earnings. So far as the more degraded women in eastern and southeastern Europe—Poland, Roumania, and elsewhere—are concerned, the earnings would probably be from five to ten times as much. On the other hand, the opportunities of their securing any material share of their earnings for their own uses is no greater, possibly not so great.

With this class of women the women procurers are probably almost as successful as the men. They call the attention of the girls to the attractiveness of a voyage abroad, to the new and interesting experiences to be met with in a new country, and especially to the greatly increased earnings and the consequent opportunities to gratify their desires for luxury and display.

RECRUITING OF INNOCENT GIRLS.

To the innocent girls the woman procurer has only the inducement of work, and usually work of a menial nature, though at higher pay than that to which the girl has been accustomed at home. In one instance a girl left her home in Europe with the consent of her parents to act as maid to the woman procurer; and there are doubtless numerous instances in which women, sometimes those of a better class, such as nurses, are offered good positions at high pay.

The investigation leads the commission to the belief, however, that more of the recruiting of innocent young girls in Europe is done by men procurers than by women; and possibly even with the women of the professional class they may be somewhat more successful, as while they can promise just as much in the way of pleasure and pay as can the woman procurer, they can also probably lead the woman to believe that they can assure them better protection and a greater security in the evasion of the law.

Correspondence captured in raids instituted by agents of the commission shows some of these methods of recruiting. These letters are extremely valuable "human documents" relating to persons of the class in question. The men seem to feel affection for their children; they talk tenderly with reference to the fortunes or misfortunes of their mothers or relatives; they send polite greetings to one another and to their friends. At the same time they discuss the characteristics of the women in question with the same coolness that they would name the good points of a horse or a blooded dog which they have for sale.

An absolutely new number—tall, handsome of figure and body, 20 years and 6 months old. She wants to earn money.[a]

The brother of Antoine and Pierre, nicknamed, "dealers in live stock." I do not want to ask any favors of them; they are great rascals.

A woman the like of whom you can never find; young, beautiful, most * * * and who fully decided to leave. You can well understand I gave them a song and dance. * * * Without praising her highly, she is as beautiful as it is possible to find in this world, and I hope she will serve your purpose well. * * * I will send you her photograph. Her beautiful teeth alone are worth a million.

Far more pitiful, however, are the cases of the innocent girls. A French girl seized in a raid of a disorderly house in Chicago stated to the United States authorities that she was approached when she was but 14 years of age; that her procurer promised her employment in America as a lady's maid or a companion at wages far beyond any that she could ever hope to get in France; that she came with him to the United States, and upon her arrival in Chicago was sold into a house of ill fame.

The testimony taken in a typical case in Seattle in 1909 shows some of the methods used in recruiting their victims by those engaged in the traffic. Flattery, promises of work, love-making, promise of marriage to a wealthy person, seduction without marriage, kind treatment for a month or two, then travel with the procurer as wife, continual deception, then an explanation to a girl of only 17 of the life awaiting her, which in her innocence she could not understand, then experience in a house of ill fame in Montreal, Canada, then personal brutality, even physical violence, taking every cent of the hard-earned money, transportation to Vancouver, to Prince Rupert, to Alaska, and to Seattle, in every city forced to earn money in a shameful life, with total earnings of more than $2,000, none of which she was able to retain, then release by arrest and readiness to be deported if only the story of her shame can be

---

[a] See Appendix III-A for letters in full.

kept from father and mother, sisters and brothers. This is but one of many such cases.[a]

Edwin W. Sims, United States district attorney in Chicago, makes the following statement, the evidence for which is on file in his office:

The hirelings of this traffic are stationed at certain points of entry in Canada where large numbers of immigrants are landed to do what is known in their parlance as "cutting-out work." In other words, these watchers for human prey scan the immigrants as they come down the gangplank of a vessel which has just arrived and "spot" the girls who are unaccompanied by fathers, mothers, brothers, or relatives to protect them. The girl who has been spotted as a desirable and unprotected victim is properly approached by a man who speaks her language and is immediately offered employment at good wages, with all expenses to the destination to be paid by the man. Most frequently laundry work is the bait held out, sometimes housework or employment in a candy shop or factory.

The object of the negotiations is to "cut out" the girl from any of her associates and to get her to go with him. Then the only thing is to accomplish her ruin by the shortest route. If she can not be cajoled or enticed by the promises of an easy time, plenty of money, fine clothes, and the usual stock of allurements—or a fake marriage—then harsher methods are resorted to. In some instances the hunters really marry their victims.

As to the sterner methods, it is, of course, impossible to speak explicitly beyond the statement that intoxication and drugging are often resorted to as a means to reduce the victims to a state of helplessness, and sheer physical violence is a common thing.

Those who recruit women for immoral purposes watch all places where young women are likely to be found under circumstances which will give them a ready means of acquaintance and intimacy, such as employment agencies, immigrant homes, moving-picture shows, dance halls, sometimes waiting rooms in large department stores, railroad stations, manicuring and hairdressing establishments. The men watching such places are usually suave in manner, well dressed, and prosperous looking. They become acquainted as intimately as possible with the young aliens, then use every conceivable method of betraying them.

Many of the girls now engaged in prostitution have told agents of the commission of the desire of procurers and disorderly-house keepers to obtain innocent young girls. They consider them particularly desirable because they have no pimp to demand a share of their earnings or to remove them from the disorderly house at will, and they will last longer, and therefore be more profitable. The proprietor of such a house will even pay a large price for such a girl. Among the papers taken from the Dufaur house, Chicago, in June, 1908, was a letter from a man in London asking Dufaur to send $200 for the passage of himself and woman from London to Chicago, and a receipt showing that the money had been received from Dufaur.

Another letter was from a woman in Brussels addressed to Mr. and Mrs. Dufaur asking if they had a place for the writer's 18-year-old sister who wished to come to America.[b] Still other evidence showed that Dufaur had paid $1,000 for an exceptionally attractive girl.

---

[a] This testimony is filed in the office of the Commissioner of Immigration at Washington. A copy containing the more essential points is found in Appendix 3B.

[b] These letters are on file in the office of the United States district attorney in Chicago.

IV.

METHODS OF IMPORTATION.

METHODS OF BOOKING.

When women are brought into the country for immoral purposes, usually they come either as wives or relatives of men accompanying them; as maids or relatives of women accompanying them; as women entering alone, booked to friends or relatives or to a home, and representing themselves as looking for work; as wives coming to men supposed to be their husbands or, in the case of Japanese, their proxy husbands.[a]

As explained in the note, some Japanese women doubtless come to this country to meet their proxy husbands when their purposes are entirely legal and proper; but it can be readily seen how liable the custom is to abuse, and in the opinion of the immigrant inspectors a large majority of the women coming in this way are intended for purposes of prostitution. If, however, the marriage ceremony is duly performed, the officials feel that nothing more can be done. It is practically impossible to prove the intention before the fact.

Some light is shed on the methods employed by Japanese in two letters from persons in Japan to men in Portland, Oreg., in 1908. (See Appendix IV–I A.)

Chinese women can enter this country under the law only when appearing as wives or daughters of the Chinese men who are of the admitted classes, such as merchants, students, travelers, government officials. Doubtless in many instances women are brought in as wives of members of these exempt classes, and are then sold to keepers of houses. Under the conditions ruling in the Chinese quarters of our cities, such women become really slaves; doubtless in many cases they have been slaves at home. Unless they are redeemed through

---

[a] In both China and Japan it is a well-known custom for marriage to be arranged by the parents or trusted relatives or friends of the contracting parties without the parties having seen each other before the ceremony. In fact, in many localities in certain social circles it is considered scarcely proper for the contracting parties to have had any personal acquaintance before the marriage. In Japan, if for any reason it is not convenient for both of the parties to be present at the marriage ceremony, one or both of them may be represented by a friend standing as his proxy. It is a custom for Japanese men residing in the United States thus to contract marriages with women in Japan, they sending their photographs and receiving those of their intended brides, so that they have in this way a picture acquaintance. The marriage is then consummated in Japan by a friend of the groom taking the pledges for the husband. This marriage is legal under the Japanese law. When such a marriage has been contracted, the bride comes to America to meet her husband, whom she has known before only by reputation and whom she has seen only by photograph. It is a custom in at least several of the United States ports for the immigration authorities to require a marriage under the laws of the United States before the woman married in this way is permitted to land. Persons familiar with the Japanese law have in many instances argued that this second marriage under the laws of the United States gives no additional validity to the marriage, and that the insistence upon such a second marriage is disrespectful to a sister nation. On the other hand, the immigration authorities have felt that this, at any rate, secured a legal marriage in certain cases where, without such a ceremony, it might well be that the woman was being imported for the purposes of prostitution. To give additional security in such cases it is necessary to insist that the alleged husband shall be able to establish his good standing in the American city in which he lives.

purchase by some man who is ready to marry them their position is practically that of permanent slavery, although theoretically they are allowed in certain instances to earn the money for the purchase of their liberty. Under the methods of exploitation followed in Chinese houses, as well as those kept by others, such self-purchase is, however, almost, if not quite, impossible.

A plan followed frequently in importing Japanese women for immoral purposes is to marry them upon their arrival to Japanese men whose status as native Americans has been established. In some instances Americans pretend to marry Japanese girls in Japan and bring them into America as their wives. Doubtless these cases are rare.

In the majority of the cases investigated by the agents of the commission the women imported in violation of section 3 of the immigration law traveled second class on the steamers, with the exception sometimes of Chinese and Japanese. The reasons for the selection of the second class of passage are: First, the saving of expense, and second, the less likelihood of detection, since their appearance would often show that they were out of place in the first cabin.

Shrewd importers do not usually bring in alien women and girls on third-class tickets, because the inspection of third-class passengers on both railroads and steamers is stricter than that of second and first class passengers, although the law is the same for all. Every alien woman entering for the first time, traveling alone third class, booked for New York, is supposed to be detained at Ellis Island until she is called for by some relative or friend. If the relative or friend fails to appear, the woman is then often discharged to one of the immigrant homes which assumes the responsibility of finding her friends or of assisting her to find a suitable place to live. If she is booked to any place outside of New York or its immediate vicinity she is seldom detained for further inquiry.

The examination of manifests at Ellis Island by the agents of the commission proved that earlier many women who gave as addresses well-known disorderly houses in the city of New York had been admitted without serious difficulty; also several women who were booked for Seattle and San Francisco, and gave addresses in the districts where the prostitutes lived. It is plain that within the last one or two years there has been much greater care taken in this regard.

A letter addressed to a member of the commission from an employee of the immigration service in the Department of Commerce and Labor gives a list of 25 women whose baggage was sent to one of the best known French resorts—the s)-called French Club, at 124 West Twenty-ninth street—although the passengers themselves were often manifested to other places. In September, 1907, the character of the house became clearly known, and since then such manifestings have ceased. The house was broken up at the time the Immigration Commission closed its investigation. (See Appendix IV–A for copy of letter.)

MARRIAGE TO AMERICAN CITIZENS.

In certain cases where there seemed some doubt regarding admission, the immigration authorities have permitted women who may technically at least be subject to deportation under the law to remain in this country if they marry American citizens. In some instances the woman has been allowed to stay if she married the person to whom she was booked, even though the man was a foreigner. There is every reason to believe that this device is followed by professional prostitutes who have no intention whatever of giving up their practices or of making a home for the man whom they marry. Presumably in many such instances the man is himself a pimp, and is taking the risk of bigamy, having already been married. Some striking instances of this kind are given in affidavits taken from the last annual report of the commissioner of police of the city of New York, and printed in Appendix IV–B.

DIFFICULTIES OF DETECTION.

It is often extremely difficult to prove the illegal entrance of either women or procurers. The inspector has to judge mainly by their appearance and the stories they tell. Two French procurers and pimps bringing girls with them were, in 1908, detained at Ellis Island because they claimed to be chauffeurs and appeared to be entering in violation of the contract-labor law. At length, however, they were allowed to land, and went direct to the French headquarters named above, telling the story to their fellow-criminals, and joking at the expense of the immigration officials.

On the Canadian border some two years ago an immigration inspector stopped by mistake the wife of a prominent citizen of one of our leading commercial cities, a woman against whose character suspicion had never been raised. The inspector was judging merely by her appearance and manner in replying to his questions. Fortunately the inspector in charge learned her name and standing before she was given the reason for her detention. An excuse was made, with a polite apology for the inconvenience caused, and she went on, not knowing why she had been stopped. If such mistakes were committed frequently, the service would soon be discredited. An inspector is not likely to run the risk. The possibility of such mistakes permits almost any reasonably well-behaved woman with some ingenuity in framing skillful answers to the usual inquiries to enter the United States, whatever her character. The higher the social standing the woman seems to have, the more cautious the inspector is about causing her unnecessary delay and trouble.

In Appendix IV–C are given other cases showing the difficulty of discovering the prostitute, and indicating the need of attempting to follow up in many instances cases that have seemed doubtful to the immigration authorities.

DIFFICULTY OF DETERMINING MODE OF PROCEDURE.

In addition to the difficulty of detecting those who are violating the law is the difficulty of determining under some circumstances the best course of action. There was the case of a Norwegian, resident in one of our northwestern cities for seven years, who had acquired property valued at several thousand dollars and had taken out his first naturalization papers. His wife died leaving him two young daughters. He returned to Norway, and brought back with him a young woman whom he declared he intended to marry after reaching his home in the West. At the port of entry it was discovered that the woman was pregnant. The man stated that they had not been married in Norway because of the difficulty of proving at that distance the death of his wife and of securing necessary papers. The woman, examined separately, confirmed his story throughout, and also said that she expected to be married as soon as they reached his home. The immigration officials had to decide whether either of these parties should be debarred from landing and whether the woman was being imported for immoral purposes. The man acknowledged that he had purshased her ticket and was paying her expenses. They held that if proof could be furnished by telegraph that the man was a widower, as alleged, and apparently a respectable citizen in the community in which he lived, and if the couple would be married in the presence of the immigration authorities, they might be admitted.

Some of the correspondence captured show the care taken by the importers in dressing their women well, in coaching the girls regarding the people to whom they are booked as relatives, and also the great care taken by the alleged relatives, on their arrival, to make their stories meet. In Appendix IV–D is given such a letter, together with a copy of the examination of the case at Ellis Island. The reading of this case, in connection with the fact that the information contained in the letter had already been called to the attention of the Commissioner of Immigration at Ellis Island, would seem to show in that particular case either a notable laxity on the part of the board of inquiry or some carelessness in reporting to the board the suspicious circumstances under which the alien was coming.

In fact, the great difficulty of enforcing the law is shown by the evidence given. It would seem imperative that the immigration officials not merely question the persons concerned in the suspected cases, but also trace afterwards a certain number of cases, from time to time, in order to familiarize themselves somewhat better with the character of certain employment agencies and other places of doubtful character. The Bureau of Immigration has already taken some steps in this direction, but it would seem very desirable that at our leading ports of entry there be kept lists brought up to date of the most noteworthy houses and even of the best-known streets where the business of prostitution is conducted, not merely in New York, but in a number of the leading cities of the country. Of course it would be comparatively easy to evade the law by giving still other addresses and booking the people to other near-by small towns. But the only remedy for the existing state of affairs is the possibility of lessening the extent of the evil by eternal vigilance and by the vigorous prosecution of the cases found. Its absolute eradication is hardly to be expected.

In order to test this matter of deception the agents of the Immigration Commission traced as best they could 65 alien women who arrived at New York from Europe in January, 1908. The results were as follows: Thirty were found to be living under proper conditions; 9 were traced to the address given on the manifest, but had moved; 5 could not be found, as no address was given on the manifest; 8 more could not be found, because the numbers given were not correct; 9 addresses given were tried, but the girls could not be located, the people of the house having never heard of them; 3 of the girls found were living under very suspicious conditions, namely: One Irish girl was booked to a Greek; a Russian girl was booked to a man alleged to be her uncle, but later found to be no relative of hers—the man was a typical Jew pimp, and refused to give the girl's present address; a Polish girl, 19 years of age, came with a man who married her just before she sailed, but who already had a wife in this country.

V.

SYSTEM OF EXPLOITATION.

METHODS OF PLACING GIRL.

The strongest appeal to the instincts of humanity in every right-minded person is made by a consideration of the brutal system employed by these traffickers in every way to exploit their victims, the hardened prostitute as well as the innocent maiden. The methods probably are not essentially different in the houses of prostitution filled with American girls, or on the part of the pimps who are exploiting them, from that obtaining in houses filled with foreign girls lately imported, or the foreign women on the streets whose knowledge of English is barely enough to enable them to give an invitation. It is probable that a somewhat larger proportion of the American girls are free from the control of a master; and yet, according to the best evidence obtainable—according to the stories of the women themselves and the keepers of houses—nearly all the women now engaged in this business in our large cities are subject to pimps to whom they give most of their earnings, or else they are under the domination of keepers of houses, a condition which is practically the same.

As has been already intimated, the motive dominating the procurer and pimp is that of commercial profit; the first thing to be done when a woman is imported is to place her where she can make money for him quickly and plentifully. The man or woman bringing her into the country may—

Take her with him to a lodging house or boarding house where he lives, engaging another room elsewhere where she may take men.

Put her into a disorderly house. If the house is not his own, he usually shares profits with the manager and reserves the right to remove his woman.

Sell her to the keeper of a disorderly house, or to a pimp, or to some intermediary.

Turn her over to his principal, if he has been acting merely as agent.

It is the business of the man who controls the woman to provide police protection, either by bribing the police not to arrest her, or in case of arrest to secure bail, pay the fine, etc., to make all business arrangements, to decide what streets, restaurants, dance halls, saloons, and similar places she shall frequent. If she is a foreigner, she is taught where to solicit, what expressions to use, where to take her men, how much to charge, and other like information. Above all, she is compelled to learn that she must give all her earnings to her man, and receive neither protection nor help from anyone else, and especially never to betray her man. As a precaution, he seldom tells her his real name, giving her only the name by which the police or his fellows know him—as "Red Sam," "Blink." The French have often very expressive titles, such as "Albert le Belge," "Louis L'Escalier," "Henri le Juif," "Frederick le Voleur," "George le Tête de Veau," "Carl le Terreur des Jeunes Filles," and "Maurice le Cocher."

The woman is told where she can find her pimp in case of need, at club, saloon, or gambling room; and she knows, of course, the place which stands for her home. She is expected every night to give him all her earnings. In some instances she is placed under the care of a woman of experience who teaches her the trade. She is invariably warned of the danger of deportation and instructed what lies to tell if she is arrested, in order to avoid deportation.

A young girl when first entering the life is very likely soon to become pregnant. Frequently, usually perhaps, abortion is performed. Otherwise she is usually compelled to continue her work as long as possible; then, after discharge from a hospital, to give her child to a foundling asylum.[a] If she tries to leave her man and get legitimate work, usually he threatens her by saying that he will tell her employer what her life has been—a measure sufficient to cause the loss of her place. Sometimes he beats her. If she betrays him, sometimes he kills her. This is the history of many alien girls, some scores of whom have been interviewed by the commission's agents in courts, in penal institutions, and in maternity hospitals.

THE CONTROL OF THE GIRLS.

The control of the man over his girl is explained in part by her real affection for him (he has often been her first lover), by the care which he gives her, by the threats which he makes against her, by even his brutality, and often beyond that there are many things that serve to make her condition helpless and hopeless. An innocent girl often revolts bitterly against the life and refuses to submit until compulsion is used. Then for a considerable length of time the man finds it necessary to watch her carefully until at length she is "broken in"—the technical expression. After that, if she tries to escape, he may apply for aid to almost any other pimp in any city in the United States. These men are constantly traveling; they frequent the same clubs, and are in close correspondence. If she has been seen by other men they make a business of remembering her, and her photograph, in case of escape, would be sent to other places. Not only do they wish to help one another, but they wish also to impress upon their own women the difficulties and danger of attempting to escape. In many cases it appears as if the police made little effort to assist the girls; for in many cases it is their business to know every prostitute who comes to town, and they doubtless would be called upon if the girl felt that they would be of assistance. Instead of feeling safe with the police they are usually threatened with the police by their pimps and sometimes they are arrested and punished on some false complaint. Not only the keepers of disorderly houses, but even saloon keepers and the keepers of the "hotels" patronized by people of this class, naturally side with the men. All the women

---

[a] The lying-in hospital in the city of New York has on an average six unmarried immigrant women confined each week.

known by the girl are either unwilling or powerless to help her. Moreover, the alien woman is ignorant of the language of the country, knows nothing beyond a few blocks of the city where she lives, has usually no money, and no knowledge of the rescue homes and institutions which might help her. If she has been here long enough and has learned, through suffering, to become resourceful, possibly how to keep secretly a little money for herself, she has often become so nervously weakened, so morally degraded, that she can not look beyond to any better life, and apparently even loses desire for any change.

According to those best informed, a very large proportion of the pimps living in the United States are foreigners. Arrests made during the investigation of men violating section 3 include the following nationalities: Egyptian, French, Chinese, Belgian, Spanish, Japanese, Greek, Slavish, Hungarian, Italian, and Russian. The French, as a rule, import women of their own nationality. The Jews often import or harbor Russian, Austrian, Hungarian, Polish, or German women, usually doubtless of their own race. The Japanese import their own women and apparently seldom harbor others, while the Chinese import their own women, but frequently harbor Americans also.

There has been much talk in the newspapers of a great monopolistic corporation whose business it is to import and exploit these unfortunate women, trafficking in them from country to country. The commission has been unable to learn of any such corporation and does not believe in its existence. Doubtless the importers and pimps have a wide acquaintance among themselves, and doubtless in many instances they have rather close business relations one with another; and inasmuch as all are criminals anyone escaping arrest can naturally appeal to another anywhere in the country for protection. Even a pimp whom he has never seen will give him shelter if he comes with a proper introduction. There are two organizations of importance, one French, the other Jewish, although as organizations they do not import. Apparently they hate each other; but their members would naturally join forces against the common enemy.

In several cities there are French headquarters—that is, a meeting place where the French importers, procurers, and pimps congregate, receive their mail, transact business, drink, gamble, and amuse themselves in other ways. Through these mutual acquaintanceships, sustained by common interests and a knowledge of their common affairs, they assist one another in the business. Sometimes small groups of individuals are organized to assist one another for a time, each going abroad in turn to send or bring girls into the United States. One combination discovered was formed between a fugitive from justice in Paris, a man in Seattle, and another in Chicago, the man in Paris supplying girls to the Northwest through Seattle and Chicago. Six of the foreigners deported from New York for violation of section 3 of the immigration act during the period of the investigation had criminal records abroad. One had been a life convict for murder in a French penal colony.

There are large numbers of Jews scattered throughout the United States, although mainly located in New York and Chicago, who seduce and keep girls. Some of them are engaged in importation, but apparently they prey rather upon young girls whom they find on the street, in the dance halls, and similar places, and whom, by the methods already indicated—love-making and pretenses of marriage— they deceive and ruin. Many of them are petty thieves, pickpockets, and gamblers. They have also various resorts where they meet and receive their mail, transact business with one another, and visit. Perhaps the best-known organization of this kind throughout the country was one legally incorporated in New York in 1904 under the name of the New York Independent Benevolent Association.[a]

As stated in their certificate of incorporation, the objects were benevolent, providing for a weekly payment to sick members and for burial. They had a cemetery lot in Flatbush where members were buried. According to the information received, the main object of the association was to assist its members, many of whom were keepers of disorderly houses, pimps, or procurers, in carrying on their business, and especially in defeating the law. When one was arrested for committing a crime, money was raised to assist him. Money was raised also for protection fees. Although the organization did not import women, many of its members did. They had regular meetings in New York City for the transaction of business, but their members were widely scattered, even as far as Victoria and Vancouver. The following is a copy of a printed card sent to members to attend the funeral of a well-known prostitute who had been murdered. Talk among the pimps and prostitutes in resorts in the neighborhood in the presence of one of our agents showed that the people of her class believed that she had been murdered because she had discarded her pimp.

NEW YORK INDEPENDENT BENEVOLENT ASSOCIATION.

BROTHER: You are requested to attend the funeral to our deceased sister, Katie Polta, which will take place on Wednesday, April 15, 1908, at 1 o'clock sharp, from the morgue, Twenty-sixth street.
For not attending, $2 fine.
By order of the president:

J. SCHLIFKA, *Secretary.*

The procurers and pimps of other nationalities are fewer in number, and the commission has not discovered regularly organized clubs among them, although doubtless they have their meeting places. There seems to be a number of Italian pimps scattered throughout the country who are apparently vicious and criminal. They at times have in their control women of other nationalities, and some of them seem to be more feared by their women than those of other nationalities.

THE WOMEN IN THE HOUSES.

When the alien woman does not live with her man nor solicit upon the streets, she usually becomes an inmate of a disorderly house, being often placed there by her man who himself receives her share of her earnings. In the house she undergoes, of course, the same treatment as that which the native woman receives, with even less opportunity of defending herself, because of her lack of knowledge of the language and the customs of the country. This ignorance

---

[a] The commission has a copy of the articles of incorporation of this association which would in themselves give no inkling of the nature of the corporation. The information has been secured in part from Jews who have themselves been active members of the association.

and her lack of friends make it practically impossible for her to escape. Her street clothes are often taken from her and locked up. Her jewelry is taken and not returned. The clothes supplied her can be used only in such a house. The money received from her customers is given to the manager of the house, she receiving a check for each dollar turned in. In most of the establishments discovered the woman was allowed to believe that she was credited on the books of the house with one-half of her earnings. If she were under the control of the proprietor, that remained to her credit. If she were placed there by a pimp, her share would regularly be paid to him.

From her half of her earnings are taken: The cost of importing and procuring her, her living expenses, physician's fees and medicines, fines, and her clothing for house wear.

For all these items she is charged exorbitant rates. Her half, therefore, with these items deducted, is sometimes small. Usually the keeper plays also upon her vanity if she wishes to go out of the house, supplying her with street clothes at exorbitant prices, with jewelry, and with money for spending, so as to keep her always in debt to the house, even though she is making a large sum of money Usually these women have not the gift of saving. They are not businesslike and can be readily kept in debt. They are made to believe often that if they escape without payment they will be captured, exposed, and arrested; and they are beaten and threatened, sometimes with murder, if they attempt to escape.

One girl swears that she was scared, slapped, threatened with arrest, and even with murder; that they kept all her money, never giving her any. She states further that all her letters from her mother were opened; that she had no clothes; that none were bought for her; that they took her jewelry, worth some $1,500, and never returned it; and that they had frightened her so that she told an inquiring policeman that she was well treated.[a]

In many cases the inmate of a disorderly house, like the prostitute who lives with her pimp, becomes so weakened and degraded that she has no desire to lead a respectable life thereafter. In Appendix V–A are printed several letters seized in raids upon these houses or handed to our agents which show clearly the workings of the system.

Mr. Harry A. Parkin, assistant United States district attorney in Chicago, makes the following statement, based upon evidence filed in the Chicago office:

In one of the recent raids a big Irish girl was taken and held as a witness. She was old enough, strong enough, and wise enough, it seemed to me, to have overcome almost every kind of opposition, even physical violence. She could have put up a fight which few men, no matter how brutal, would care to meet. I asked her why she did not get out of the house, which was one of the worst in Chicago. Her answer was: "Get out! I can't. They make us buy the cheapest rags, and they are charged against us at fabulous prices; they make us change outfits at intervals of two or three weeks, until we are so deeply in debt that there is no hope of ever getting out from under. Then, to make such matters worse, we seldom get an accounting oftener than once in six months, and sometimes ten months or a year will pass between settlements, and when we do get an accounting it is always to find ourselves deeper in debt than before. We've simply got to stick, and that's all there is to it." [b]

---

[a] This evidence was secured from the United States district attorney in Chicago.

[b] Still other cases of a similar nature are printed in Appendix V–B. The proof of these statements is in part filed in the office of the United States district attorney in Chicago and is partly on the authority of one of the commission's agents.

Besides statements made by the women themselves to agents of the commission, many similar instances come to the notice of prosecuting officers wherever such cases are brought before them. In the note following is an affidavit from the assistant district attorney in Chicago covering several of these statements made to him:

STATE OF ILLINOIS, *County of Cook, ss:*

Harry A. Parkin, being first duly sworn, on oath deposes and says that he is an assistant United States attorney for the northern district of Illinois; that during the month of June, 1908, he was assigned to Edward W. Sims, United States attorney for said district, to assist him in the so-called "white slave" investigations; that as part of his duties he has examined many keepers and inmates of houses of prostitution; that from statements made to him it is safe to say that at that time it was the practice in very many houses of prostitution in Chicago to compel the inmates to purchase their clothing from the keepers of the respective houses or through them of some particular merchant; that the prices charged for such articles were approximately three or four times the actual market value of the respective articles. That upon several occasions girls have exhibited certain wearing apparel to him which they said they had purchased from the keepers of the houses of which they were inmates, and have told him the prices paid for the same. These articles included stockings which would sell in the open market for not to exceed 75 cents per pair, and which the girl stated she had paid for at the rate of $3 per pair; that shoes worth from $2.50 to $3.50 per pair were charged against the girls at from $7 to $8 per pair; that house wrappers or kimonos worth not to exceed $4 to $5 were charged at $12 to $15.

HARRY A. PARKIN.

Subscribed and sworn to before me this 7th day of September, A. D. 1909.

WILLIAM A. SMALL,
Notary Public in and for Cook County, Ill.

Illustrative of the unspeakable brutality manifested in deception, threats, physical cruelty, even to the extent of criminal assaults, and in the demands for submission to degrading practices even worse than that of ordinary prostitution, is the testimony printed in Appendix V-C, taken in Seattle from an alien woman subject to deportation under section 3 of the immigration act. While the case is itself of a type that is not frequent, still it is typical. The original is on file in the Department of Commerce and Labor. Not merely is it in itself complete in description, but all the inspectors and attorneys connected with the prosecution were of the opinion that every statement made by the witness was strictly true.

VI.

INTERSTATE AND LOCAL CONDITIONS.

The importation and exploitation of alien women is doubtless affected very materially by local conditions, economic and administrative. The agents of the commission learned, for example, that whereas formerly the city of Buffalo used to be a considerable center for the importation of women from Canada, under the present administration the laws against the practice of prostitution were so rigorously enforced that that city was no longer a desirable port of entry. In consequence, when women were brought across from Canada at that port, they generally did not stop in the city but went immediately beyond to some interior point.

At the time of the commission's investigation in New York it was almost impossible for the procurers to find a satisfactory place in any house of prostitution for a woman imported in violation of section 3.

The reason for this was that many houses were closed because of raids and fear of investigation; that those still remaining open were run on a small scale, so that the demand for girls was light; and that the houses, especially those where aliens were formerly placed, were continually raided. The effect of this activity upon the houses was that many of the most notorious keepers, especially Frenchmen, had left the city, and were doing business in the cities of the West, where the dangers were not so great; that nearly all of the alien women brought to New York were living with their pimps instead of in disorderly houses; and that a large proportion of these aliens were soliciting on the street rather than remaining in the houses. All of these practices tended to affect quite decidedly the custom of importation, if not its extent.

The continual raiding of the houses in the so-called "tenderloin" and other well-known districts had beyond question scattered the practice of prostitution from these houses into tenement houses and small apartment houses throughout the city.

Some of the clubs at which the procurers stopped on their travel to and from Europe still remained open. One of the best known was raided as a result of the investigation made by the commission, and several hundred letters were found there addressed to procurers and pimps throughout the country, letters which had apparently come from all parts of the world. Most of them mentioned facts which indicated that the business between the correspondents would constitute a violation of the immigration law.

It is, of course, difficult to prove by specific cases the relation of the police to this traffic and to establish by specific evidence the fact generally accepted that the girls and disorderly house keepers regularly pay the police for protection; but high police officials, prosecuting officers, and social workers in all quarters assert that in many, if not all, of our large cities much corruption of this kind exists. Most of the girls questioned by the commission's agents on this point said that payments were made to the police to insure their protection from too frequent arrests. It is, of course, a violation of the law for the police to demand or receive such money; but the woman who did not pay for protection was frequently arrested. The woman who did pay was sometimes arrested when the policeman must "make good" at headquarters. When the women understood this situation, they did not complain. When a police officer, a plain-clothes man, was shifted, he naturally felt obliged to make arrests. Under the circumstances he would, of course, arrest the women to whom he was under no obligations.

When a house of prostitution was raided, the police usually did not bring the woman practicing prostitution to the court. They arrested instead the woman ostensibly managing the house. The real proprietor is comparatively seldom found within reach of arrest, although he pays the fine and furnishes bail.

The women arrested for practicing prostitution or for soliciting on the streets and brought into the magistrate's court in New York City soon learned to know, or her man did for them, the temper of each magistrate. For example, they knew that one magistrate would release all women without fines, another would place them on probation, a third would send them to the workhouse, a fourth would fine them $2, and a fifth would invariably fine them $10. It was a matter of common knowledge when a certain magistrate would be sitting. The severe judge had few cases—women paid more to the police or kept out of sight when he was holding court—and the lenient one had his court room filled every evening. In the latter case women were arrested frequently, sometimes twice in one month. It was a common occurrence for women to be placed on probation, even though they had previously served several times in the work-house. So quickly were cases disposed of that many women within ten minutes after being brought into the court were placed on probation and had disappeared, not to be heard from until the next time they were arrested. Sometimes from 50 to 100 of these cases were disposed of in one night.

Any investigation of local conditions is unsatisfactory, because the exploitation of women in a given locality at any particular time is controlled by financial, political, and social conditions. The men and women who exploit women for purposes of prostitution are quick to note, even to anticipate, changes in these conditions and to adjust their business to them. Therefore the pimps, the disorderly-house keepers, and the prostitutes controlled by them move frequently from place to place, being actuated by fear of arrest, or by the hope of making large profits.

In Appendix VI–A are given a number of letters which make clear the points here indicated.

VII.

PROFITS OF THE TRAFFIC.

In naming the business of importing women the "white slave traffic" the public has instinctively stated the fact that the business is maintained for profit. It is probably no exaggeration to say that if means can be devised of stripping the profits from it the traffic will cease.

While many thousands of people are making a good living out of this business, it would be too much to say that large fortunes are derived directly from it. The large sums, frequently though not regularly made, are often quickly squandered in gambling and dissipation. The belief that a single corporation is largely controlling this traffic in the United States is doubtless a mistake. The number of women imported by any one person or organization is probably quite limited. It has been estimated by United States District Attorney Sims that one man engaged in the traffic who forfeited two bonds of $25,000 each for himself and wife was probably worth some $87,000. So far as can be learned, he was the wealthiest of the importers in Chicago at the time of the investigation there. He also was a disorderly-house keeper and probably derived the largest profits from the use of his girls rather than from selling them; his profits might have been large, although probably not so large, if his girls had been native-born Americans instead of imported.

The rules governing the profits from the prostitution of women living in the United States in violation of section 3 of the immigration act are those governing the profits in any business in that—

A woman is worth to her procurer the price for which he sells her, less the cost to him of recruiting and importing her.

A woman is worth to the pimp, or disorderly-house keeper (where he is also her procurer), the amount of her earnings less (a) the cost of importing or recruiting her, or her purchase price; (*b*) cost of her support; (*c*) expenses of the business.

The data secured as to the amounts made in the business show that profits vary with the locality where the traffic is carried on, with fluctuations in social, financial, and political conditions, with the personality of the alien, and with the nationality and business ability of her exploiter.

To guard against the sensational beliefs that are becoming prevalent, it is best to repeat that the agents of this commission have not learned that all or even the majority of the alien women and girls practicing prostitution in the United States in violation of the immigration act were forced or deceived into the life; that they have not learned that all who entered the life unwillingly or unknowingly are desirous of leaving it; and they have not proved that alien women as a class are more quickly degraded than native women, though from their ignorance of the language and customs they are at times less able to guard themselves. Moreover, since in Europe the feeling regarding sexual immorality is much less pronounced than in the United States, the women presumably in many instances have not the consciousness of degradation from their fallen condition that in some instances causes the American girl her keenest suffering.

They have learned that a large number of alien women and girls is being imported (sometimes unwillingly, but usually willingly) into the United States and distributed throughout the several States for the purposes of prostitution; that alien women and girls in considerable numbers have been so deceived or taken advantage of by procurers that they have found themselves in conditions which practically forced them into practicing prostitution; and that all of those engaged in the exploitation of these alien women or girls use every means of degrading them, in order to keep them in the life as long as they are able to earn money.

Often the lure to the women is evidently not more in the amount of money made than in the apparent ease and excitement of making it. Even the smallest profits made in the exploitation of women are, however, sufficient to tempt the man who is willing to be supported by a woman's shame in order that he may be free to drink or gamble, and to tempt the woman who has no desire to earn an honest livelihood.

It is obvious that the qualities required for the securing of these profits are the daring and shrewdness of the criminal rather than the energy and industry necessary for success in a legitimate business.

THE PRICE OF GIRLS.

It is of course impossible to state any regular price that is paid for girls, or the regular expenses of importing and placing them. The traffic is largely individual with both the importer and the girl, and the cost varies materially.

The expressions "buying girls," "selling girls," etc., also vary in meaning. In order to test the assertions frequently made regarding the ease with which girls could be "bought" at employment agencies for such purposes or could be secured through employment agencies for work as servants in disorderly houses, agents of the commission applied to certain employment agencies asking for girls to work in disorderly houses. Girls were delivered by employment agencies to a room hired for the purpose of making the test, for the payment of a $5 fee or even less; but in cases like this the employment agent is in no proper sense "selling" the girl. He is simply paid a fee for his work as an agent, though he is doing a vile business.

On the other hand, testimony shows that when an importer sells a girl to a disorderly house keeper or to a pimp, and frequently into what is practically slavery, he often receives $500 or more, in certain cases twice or three times that sum; an amount sufficient to cover the expense to which he has been put in securing the girl, his own expenses, and a substantial profit. The following affidavit gives a specific instance of this kind;

STATE OF ILLINOIS, *County of Cook, ss.*

———— ————, first being sworn on oath, deposes and says that during the months of October, November, and December, 1908, and January and February, 1909, he was employed as a special investigator by the Immigrátion Commission; that as part of his duties he investigated the purchase and sale of women for immoral purposes in Chicago and elsewhere, with particular reference to women of French nationality; that in these investigations statements were made by a certain keeper of a house of prostitution in Chicago that for a certain French girl named Marcelle he had paid the sum of $1,000; that for a certain French girl named Mascotta, who was an inmate of his house, he had paid the sum of $500 and a like sum for another girl whose name he does not remember; that a certain girl named Lille, also a French girl, was sent from Chicago to Omaha and sold to a keeper of a house of prostitution in that city for the sum of $1,400.

Deponent further says that Louis Paint, now an inmate of the penitentiary at Atlanta, Ga., stated to deponent that he had received the sum of $800 for two girls whom he brought from Paris, France, to Chicago and sold to a keeper of a house of prostitution in Chicago; that thereafter he was sent by the same keeper to Paris again and given $2,000 with which to procure four additional girls; that these girls were procured in Paris, brought to New York, but that they were there stopped by the immigration inspectors and the procurers arrested.

Deponent further says that he has talked with other keepers and procurers for houses of prostitution and that it is not an extraordinary thing to pay such prices for French women; that $500 is the ordinary price for a French prostitute when delivered in America, and that this price was stated to have been received by a certain procurer whenever he brought a French prostitute to Chicago.

———— ————.

Subscribed and sworn to before me this —— day of September, A. D. 1907.

———— ————.

Different still is the work of a man who as an agent lures a girl into a house where she is overpowered, or who by false stories of profit and perhaps promise of marriage seduces the girl and then delivers her in her misfortune into the hands of a keeper of a house of prostitution. Work of this kind is done sometimes for sums as low as $15. This, again, may be quite different from a sale into practical slavery, because the girl may in many cases leave the house, if she can make a friend outside or has enough independence of disposition to assert herself.

In their investigation of the Japanese procurers it was learned that Japanese girls could be secured in Seattle to be taken to houses in Chicago or New York for $400 each, with the understanding that if several girls were taken at one time the price would be somewhat less, $300. A Japanese procurer wished to have a specific contract, and the girls were to understand that they must work out the prices that were paid for them.[a] Japanese girls are frequently placed in

---

[a] See Appendices VII–A for correspondence and affidavit on this subject.

houses where their customers are men of any nation. Chinese girls, on the contrary, with very rare exceptions, are placed in houses patronized only by Chinese. Moreover, owing in part to the small number of Chinese women in the United States, and in part to the difficulty of importing Chinese women on account of the Chinese-exclusion act, the prices paid for them range from $2,000 to $3,000, or even more. It is but natural that the importer or purchaser, as a consequence, takes all precautions to lessen the likelihood of his financial loss.

Of great importance to the business is a rigid or lax enforcement of the law. When in New York City, under General Bingham, police commissioner, a determined effort was made to close the houses, the complaints throughout the Tenderloin and other disreputable districts were many and loud. Business was poor, fines were frequent and heavy. In consequence, girls by the hundreds were taken or sent by their exploiters to other cities. The agents of the commission saw in Chicago, Salt Lake City, Ogden, and elsewhere girls whom they had not known of in New York, and who stated that they had left New York on account of the poor business there. When the rigid enforcement of the law relaxes the news spreads with wonderful rapidity and the statements that the city is "wide open" mean the flocking back of this element from other States, and an increased tendency toward the violation of the laws of importation.

In shifting girls from one State or one city to another, it is customary for the disorderly-house keeper who is to receive a girl to advance her transportation. The girl has then to make money enough to pay back this loan and her own expenses. If the girl has a pimp, the balance must be sent to him.

All concerned in the exploitation of immigrant women under the system above described seem to share the profits except the immigrant girl herself. Although she earns the money at the cost of her body and soul, she is rarely able to retain anything.

Briefly stated, the distribution of the profits derived from the services of alien women in the United States, in violation of section 3 of the immigration act, is directly to the procurer, importer, purchaser, pimp, or disorderly house keeper, the receivers of fines and license fees, sometimes the police, and indirectly to the landlords, boarding-house keepers, restaurant keepers, the police, saloon keepers, physicians, and keepers of many other establishments.

During the month of October, 1908, over $5,000 was paid into the police fund in Seattle, Wash., as fines by prostitute women— each woman being fined $10 a month. A large proportion of these women were aliens. The same custom obtains in many cities. Will the profits make the taxpayers less eager to enforce the law?

The cost of a rigid enforcement of the laws is often more than paid by the procurers.

As a result of the work of this commission in its investigation into violations of section 3 of the immigration act, fines and forfeited bail were paid into the United States Treasury, through the United States district attorney at Chicago, amounting to $125,000. The pity of it is that the money to pay the fines had been earned, not by the worst criminals, but by their exploited victims.

S. Doc. 196, 61-2——3

VIII.

EFFECTS.

It is not necessary to dwell at length upon the evil effects of viola-tions of section 3 forbidding the importation of women for immoral purposes. They are evident. The women who come into the country innocent, and are placed in this business, either against their will or otherwise, enter upon a life of such physical ills and moral degradation that relatively few find it possible to regain any status of respecta-bility or comfortable living. Here and there the agents of the com-mission have found one and another who have been rescued from the slavery, others have gladly abandoned the life, a few have married, but these cases are rare. The usual history is one of increased degra-dation until death.

Of those women who are already prostitutes when they enter the country, a very large percentage, if not all, are diseased.

Those who are not physically diseased when they enter the life usu-ally soon become so. This means suffering and a shortening of life to them and a frequent transmission of the disease to others. The best experts in this field have no hesitancy in saying that as a source of physical degeneration alone these diseases are to be guarded against even more than tuberculosis, typhoid, or any of the other infectious diseases. While these diseases are common with all prostitutes, those coming from abroad, both men and women, contrary to law, are new sources of infection.

The economic loss, coming from this shortening of life and from the expenditure of the large sums of money in all the multifarious ways of vice, which can not be considered even indirectly productive econom-ically, but which rather are mere waste from practically every point of view, is great.

It is unnecessary to comment on the ruinous influence of prosti-tution upon domestic and social life, or on its horrible effects which come alike to the guilty and the innocent. But the horrors of the evil are accentuated and its practices made more terrible in their results by the importation of women for purposes of prostitution, with its attendant system of brutal degeneracy and cruel slavery.

Both from the investigations of the commission and those of the Bureau of Immigration, it is clear that there is a beginning, at any rate, of a traffic in boys and men for immoral purposes. The same measures employed for the restriction of the traffic in women should be applied with even greater rigidity, if possible, in the cases of men, and our laws should be so amended as to apply to all persons engaged in immoral practices.

The need of checking this importation is especially great. The vilest practices are brought here from continental Europe, and be-yond doubt there has come from imported women and their men the most bestial refinements of depravity. The inclination of the con-tinental races to look with toleration upon these evils is spreading in this country an influence perhaps even more far-reaching in its degra-dation than the physical effects which inevitably follow it.

IX.

RECOMMENDATIONS.

Owing to the difference between the European and American views regarding prostitution, cooperation for the suppression of the white slave traffic can be expected from most of the European nations only along certain lines. Most European countries are rigid in their regulations regarding the procuring for purposes of prostitution of minor girls or of any women by means of fraud and deceit. Women who are of age, however, and who enter the business of their own accord are not interfered with. From continental countries where these conditions exist practically no cooperation could be expected to prevent the sailing of professional prostitutes to the United States. They probably would cooperate to prevent the seduction of minors or the fraudulent or forcible exportation of their women. In the main, however, the United States Government must rely upon its own officials for the prevention of this traffic.

In view of the conditions shown in the preceding report, it is clear that the recommendations made should be of two kinds:

First, those which have to do with the administrative work of the Department of Commerce and Labor, particularly of the Bureau of Immigration.

Second, those requiring new legislation.

In the judgment of the commission the Secretary of Commerce and Labor would do well to make the following administrative changes or to insist upon more rigid enforcement of existing regulations:

1. In carrying out the provisions of the treaty made with the leading European Governments concerning the white-slave traffic, as well as in the administration of the law excluding from this country alien criminals, there should be attached to our embassies in some of the most important countries, especially France, Great Britain, Germany, Austria, Hungary, and Italy, a special agent with authority to employ assistants who work in conjunction with foreign governments; first, in the way of securing information which might assist in the deportation of criminals and prostitutes found here; second, in the way of furnishing information which might lead to the prosecution in foreign courts of aliens for crimes committed either here or abroad, especially for inducing women to enter upon an immoral life and go to the United States to engage in immoral practices.

2. The Secretary of Commerce and Labor should direct the special agent of the Department of Commerce and Labor, who would work in foreign countries under his immediate direction, to secure information not only regarding ordinary criminals, but also regarding prostitutes or young women who are presumably being taken to the United States for immoral purposes. Such information should be in most cases given in advance to the steamship companies, so as to prevent the sailing of such persons. Provided such persons do sail, information should be furnished our immigrant officials in advance of their landing.

3. Government agents on the steamer, whose duty it is to enforce the immigration laws, should likewise be instructed to give especial attention to passengers presumably connected with the white-slave traffic.

4. Record of the maiden name of an alien woman booked as a wife, as well as the address of the nearest relative or friend of the wife, should be set out in the manifest.

Comment.—Inspection of manifests revealed the fact that seldom any record is made of the maiden name of the young alien women booked as wives, nor is any address given of their relatives or friends in their own country, and that girls have been imported for immoral purposes whose records failed to show their own addresses, or the names and addresses of their relatives or friends, the absence of which prohibited any inquiry in their own country.

5. At the chief ports of landing the matrons, as well as the members of the board of inquiry before whom cases that are presumably connected with the white-slave traffic come, should be appointed with especial reference to their ability to detect and deal with such cases.

Comment.—Our investigations show that the matrons at some of our ports say that it is not possible for them to recognize either procurers or prostitutes when they land. Of course, identification can not be certain, but persons familiar with people of this type would, in most instances, be able to see whether special care should be taken in the investigation of such cases before landing.

6. Doubtful cases of young alien women at ports of landing should be held until detailed inquiry can be made regarding the persons to whom they are to be discharged and regarding the places to which they are to be sent.

Comment.—It has been noted that persons are frequently discharged to people who are working in conjunction with procurers, and that sometimes little care has been taken to determine relationships between the passenger and the person to whom the passenger is discharged. Similar carelessness has often been shown with reference to the place to which the young woman is sent, the place at times being a resort well known to the police of the cities in question.

7. Every effort should be made to secure the fullest cooperation among the immigration officials at the different ports at which most criminals and prostitutes arrive.

Comment.—At present cooperation among some ports seems very complete. Inasmuch, however, as the persons deported frequently return very shortly to another port, this cooperation should be made as complete as possible.

8. The right should be given to every inspector assigned to such duty to arrest on sight any alien woman found practicing prostitution, and also any alien man who appears to be living upon her earnings or who is supporting or harboring her for immoral purposes.

Comment.—The hiding of the girls and the shifting from one city and State to another makes it very difficult to keep track of an immigrant girl practicing prostitution. Often the delay in obtaining a warrant results in the failure to find the girl when the department is ready to make the arrest.

The commission recommends that the following changes be made in the immigration laws:

1. That section 3 of the immigration act of February 20, 1907, be amended by removing the limitation of three years after the date of landing within which the prostitute or procurer must be found.

Comment.—The evils of the traffic are ordinarily not lessened with the length of time the criminal or prostitute remains in the country.

2. All persons violating the act who have been debarred or deported, if they later return to and attempt to enter the United States, should be declared guilty of misdemeanor and should be punished by imprisonment for not more than two years. and at the expiration of such term be deported.

Comment.—Under our present regulations deported prostitutes return frequently and make further efforts to enter the country, often continuing until they succeed. A penalty would probably prevent these attempts in many cases. The reentry of women once deported is apparently an easy matter. Many of them return again through the port of New York, and some enter by way of Boston, New Orleans, and Quebec. The deportation of a woman is by no means a safeguard against her returning. Many deliberately state that they will return. One prostitute has been deported several times upon information given by a man who several years ago imported her, and to whom she had become a nuisance rather than a source of income. Very frequently the fact that the girl is a prostitute is made known by some man who wishes to be rid of her. Within the month of December, 1908, a French importer, living in San Francisco, offered $500 to anyone who would bring about the deportation of a girl that he had imported two years previous, because he heard that she had intended to testify against him. Another man, whose girl had been sent to the workhouse for six months, stated to one of the agents of the commission that he intended to have her deported at once so that she would be freed of her imprisonment and enabled to return to ply her trade in a much shorter time than if she were allowed to serve her sentence. Not long ago a young girl who had been converted to the Mormon faith landed at Boston. Having admitted that she believed in polygamy, she was immediately deported and a few weeks later was found in Salt Lake City, having entered by way of Canada.

3. The penalties of perjury should be inflicted upon those taking false oath regarding the circumstances connected with these crimes.

Comment.—It is understood that under some of our laws, e. g., the Chinese exclusion act and immigration act, the penalty of perjury is not imposed for taking a false oath. Clearly, if perjury is to be recognized and punished as a crime, it should be recognized and the penalty imposed in these circumstances.

4. The burden of proof regarding the date and place of landing should be placed upon the alien, if those facts are needed.

Comment.—Under the regulations of the Bureau of Immigration, under ordinary circumstances, the burden of proof has rested upon the bureau to prove the date and place of landing. Generally speaking, no hardship would be imposed upon the criminals or prostitutes in question if they were compelled to state the time and place of landing, although under the law as amended this will generally not be necessary. The present rule in many cases defeats absolutely the purpose of the law. The new ruling would very seldom, if ever, be any hardship to any innocent person.

5. The keeping or management of any house of prostitution by an alien, or the taking of all or part of the earnings of any prostitute, should be sufficient cause for deportation of such alien.

Comment.—While the regulations regarding prostitution are ordinarily matters of state legislation, it would seem entirely fitting for the Federal Government to forbid to aliens certain acts injurious to the country under penalty of deportation if they were committed. This seems a case in point.

6. Steamship companies should be required to take back from whence they came all debarred or deported passengers in the same class of passage in which they came to this country.

Comment.—Under present circumstances it will often pay a steamship company financially to take the risk of bringing over a criminal or prostitute first or second class, taking the risk of their deportation, since if they can be returned to their own country at steerage rates a profit will be made. This possibility of securing a profit from criminals and prostitutes who are deported should be removed.

7. Cases should be prosecuted in the district where evidence is most readily secured.

8. The legislatures of the various States should be asked to enact laws requiring the detention of every alien woman convicted under the state laws of practicing prostitution, and further providing for the notification of the Department of Commerce and Labor of such cases, in order that immediate steps may be taken for the deportation of such women.

Comment.—The difficulty of locating a girl convicted of prostitution when she has been discharged, paroled, or fined suggests the advisability of this enactment.

9. The transportation of persons from any State, Territory, or District to another for the purposes of prostitution should be forbidden under heavy penalties.

10. The legislatures of the several States should consider the advisability of enacting more stringent laws regarding prostitution. It is suggested that the Illinois statute regarding pandering be carefully considered.

APPENDIXES.

Appendix I-A.

[Approved February 20, 1907.]

Sec. 3. That the importation into the United States of any alien woman or girl for the purpose of prostitution, or for any other immoral purpose, is hereby forbidden; and whoever shall, directly or indirectly, import, or attempt to import, into the United States, any alien woman or girl for the purpose of prostitution, or for any other immoral purpose, or whoever shall hold or attempt to hold any alien woman or girl for any such purpose in pursuance of such illegal importation, or whoever shall keep, maintain, control, support, or harbor in any house or other place, for the purpose of prostitution, or for any other immoral purpose, any alien woman or girl, within three years after she shall have entered the United States, shall, in every such case, be deemed guilty of a felony, and on conviction thereof be imprisoned not more than five years and pay a fine of not more than five thousand dollars; and any alien woman or girl who shall be found an inmate of a house of prostitution or practicing prostitution, at any time within three years after she shall have entered the United States, shall be deemed to be deported as provided by sections twenty and twenty-one of this act.

AGREEMENT BETWEEN THE UNITED STATES AND OTHER POWERS FOR THE REPRESSION OF THE TRADE IN WHITE WOMEN.

Article 1. Each of the contracting governments agree to establish or designate an authority who will be directed to centralize all information concerning the procuration of women or girls with a view to their debauchery in a foreign country; that the authority shall have the right to correspond directly with the similar service established in each of the other contracting states.

Art. 2. Each of the governments agree to exercise a supervision for the purpose of finding out, particularly in stations, ports of embarkation, and on the journey, the conductors of women or girls intended for debauchery. Instructions shall be sent for that purpose to the officials or to any other qualified persons, in order to procure within the limits of the laws all information of a nature to discover a criminal traffic.

The arrival of persons appearing evidently to be the authors, the accomplices, or the victims of such a traffic will be communicated in each case, either to the authorities of the place of destination, or to the interested diplomatic or consular agents, or to any other competent authorities.

Art. 3. The governments agree to receive, in each case, within the limits of the laws, the declarations of women and girls of foreign nationality who surrender themselves to prostitution, with a view to establish their identity and their civil status and to ascertain who has induced them to leave their country. The information received will be communicated to the authorities of the country of origin of said women or girls, with a view to their eventual return.

The governments agree, within the limits of the laws, and as far as possible, to confide temporarily and with a view to their eventual return the victims of criminal traffic, when they are without any resources, to some institutions of public or private charity, or to private individuals furnishing the necessary guaranties.

The governments agree also, within the limits of the laws, to return to their country of origin such of said women or girls who ask to be so returned or who may be claimed

85

by persons having authority over them. Such return will be made only after reaching an understanding as to their identity and nationality, as well as to the place and date of their arrival at the frontier. Each of the contracting parties will facilitate their transit over its territory.

Correspondence relative to the return (of such women or girls) will be made, as far as possible, through direct channels.

ART. 4. In case the woman or girl to be sent back can not herself pay the expenses of her transportation and she has neither husband, nor relations, nor guardian to pay for her the expenses occasioned by her return, they shall be borne by the country in whose territory she resides as far as the nearest frontier or port of embarkation in the direction of the country of origin, and by the country of origin for the remainder.

ART. 5. The provisions of the above articles 3 and 4 shall not infringe upon the special conventions which may exist between the contracting governments.

ART. 6. The contracting governments agree, within the limits of the laws, to exercise, as far as possible a supervision over the bureaus or agencies which occupy themselves with finding places for women or girls in foreign countries.

ART. 7. The nonsignatory states are admitted to adhere to this present arrangement. For this purpose, they shall notify their intention through diplomatic channels, to the French Government, which shall inform all the contracting states.

ART. 8. The present arrangement shall take effect six months after the date of the exchange of ratifications. In case one of the contracting parties shall denounce it, that denunciation shall take effect only as regards that party, and then twelve months only after the date of said denunciation.

ART. 9. The present arrangement shall be ratified and the ratifications shall be exchanged at Paris, as soon as possible.

In faith whereof the respective plenipotentiaries have signed the present agreement, and thereunto affixed their seals.

Done at Paris the 18th of May, 1904, in single copy which shall be deposited in the archives of the ministry of foreign affairs of the French Republic, and of which one copy, certified correct, shall be sent to each contracting party.

Signed by the representatives of the Governments of Germany, Belgium, Denmark, Spain, France, Great Britain, Italy, the Netherlands, Portugal, Russia, Sweden, Norway, and the Swiss Federal Council.

APPENDIX II.

Year of last arrival of foreign-born persons convicted in disorderly houses and soliciting cases in the night court of New York during the period November 15, 1908, to March 15, 1909, by race specified.

[This table includes those fined, held, sent to workhouse, and reprimanded.]

Race.	1908.	1907.	1906.	1905.	1904.	1903.	1902.
Canadian, French					1		
Croatian			1				
Danish						1	1
Dutch							1
English	1		4	1		3	
Finnish			1				
Flemish						1	1
French	1			17	34	28	22
German	1	1	2	2	4	4	3
Hebrew	3	2	4	7	12	19	28
Irish				2	1	1	3
Italian, north					1		1
Italian, south	1		1	3	4	1	1
Magyar	1				1	4	1
Polish		1		1			1
Scandinavian			2	1	2	1	1
Slovak		1					
Spanish							2
Swedish					1		
Total	8	5	15	34	61	63	66

Year of last arrival of foreign-born persons convicted in disorderly houses and soliciting cases in the night court of New York during the period November 15, 1908, to March 15, 1909, by race specified—Continued.

Race.	1901.	1900.	1890–1899.	1880–1889.	1870–1879.	Not reported.	Total.
African, Negro			1				1
Canadian, French							1
Croatian							1
Danish							2
Dutch	1						2
English	2	1	3	3		1	19
Finnish							1
Flemish	2			1		1	6
French	14	11	14	6	1	6	154
German	10	3	31	3		5	69
Hebrew	28	31	63	8		20	225
Irish	2	1	8	4		7	29
Italian, north		1	2				5
Italian, south	1	3	5	4		2	26
Magyar		1	1				9
Mexican			3				3
Polish		1	4	1		1	10
Scandinavian			2				9
Scotch			1	2		1	4
Slovak							1
Spanish	1						3
Swedish							1
Total	61	53	138	32	1	44	581

Appendix III–A.

The following letters, taken in various raids instituted by agents of this commission, describe methods of recruiting.

[Translation.]

PARIS, *May 5, 1907.*

MY DEAR ALBERT: At last I have succeeded in getting your address, and I hasten to write to you, not to ask anything from you, but in the first place to get the news as well as that of your woman. I notice that you have forgotten your old friend, for you had my address at Bry, but never write to me. That is sufficient rebuke. I will write you now, so you may tell me what I must do in order to leave here with an absolutely new number, tall, handsome of figure and body, 20 years and 6 months old; she wants to earn money. At present I can not buy her any new clothes, therefore she is earning nothing. For a week she entered rue St. Apoline, five days at rue Hanover, with the same result, no go; for it is evermore the old inmates who get along when there are good patrons. Since then misery has been upon us, for I found a birthday certificate, by means of which I succeeded in getting her into these houses, but fate left a red mark on her, so that in good houses she is refused. A red mark means that she has been in prison; however, she wants to do all she can to succeed. Since you are connected with houses over here, I rely upon you for giving me directions as to what I must do in this case, for I am sure she will do anything she sets her heart on in your country.

Do you know Matilda that lives in New York, the former woman of Philippe, the brother of Antoinie and Pierre, nicknamed "the dealers in live stock?" I do not want to ask any favors of them. They are great rascals. I learn at the same time that you were with Coco Bory. Give him my best regards.

In my next letter I will inform you of the misfortune that came to me with regard to my brother. For the past seven months my boy has been in Switzerland. I await your answer with impatience.

EMILE DETEINDRE,
————, *Paris.*

(Envelope: Monsieur Jean Cassardi, New York, Amérique du Nord.)

REPORT ON HARBORING WOMEN FOR IMMORAL PURPOSES.

[Translation.]

DEAR FRIEND: I take pleasure in sending you news of myself, which at the moment is most excellent.

The first time I did not have much chance to send you the woman as soon as I received your letter, because I could not attend to it myself personally, but after what we have agreed upon with Napoleon, I can assure you that I have found a woman the like of whom you can never find; young, beautiful, the most ——, and who fully decided to leave. You can well understand I gave them a song and dance. She frequents the Café ——, and, without praising her highly, she is as beautiful as it is possible to find in this world, and I hope she will serve your purpose well. As matters stand at the present moment, I could send her by the first mail steamer, so as soon as you get this letter send me the ticket or the money. If you wish, I will send her under her own name. She has all her papers, and if you send her the ticket, send it under the name of Napoleon's wife, 34 years old.

Now, my dear friend, you tell me to be very serious. You must understand that these are not matters to make light of. On the contrary, nobody knows anything about it except Napoleon, who you very well understand must be informed about it. You know that for mine and your own personal interest that I must keep this matter absolutely quiet. I will send you her photograph. Her beautiful teeth alone are worth a million. Now, my dear friend, answer me as soon as you have received my letter so that I may know what to do. Then, I have another one, but she has left for a few days and gone to Avignon; therefore, dear friend, if you decide that we do business together, it behooves you to let me know as soon as possible.

I will not detain you any longer, but will shake hands most cordially.

Your friend for life,

BAPTISTIN.

Answer soon. Accept regard of Napoleon, as well as his family.

APPENDIX III–B.

PARTIAL TESTIMONY IN A SEATTLE CASE.

Q. State now, in brief, your life history from the time you left your parents until your arrest.

A. I left my home, ——, November 1, 1906, for Paris, to work at No. ——, for a lady named ——; my father and my mother saw me to the train. I have one brother, ——, aged 20; one sister, ——, aged 22, and another sister, ——, aged 15. The oldest sister is working in Paris and the youngest is still at home.

To explain how it came that I got here, I must tell you from the beginning; how I met Emil Chaillet, or, as he calls himself now, Ernest Beretzi, the man who ruined me.

While I was employed in a delicatessen store two men called to buy something and left. I met them again on the street some time later and they asked me to be allowed to accompany me home, which I refused. Next time they met me they took me to a café and treated me. They told me they knew a man who was looking for girls to do some kind of work which paid better money than I was getting at the store, but they would not tell me what kind of work it was. They also told me that the man was very rich and asked me how I would like to marry a rich man. I told them I would like to see him first. They asked me to go with them, but I declined. They called again at the store and bought some citrons. They could not speak to me, as Mrs. ——, the lady for whom I then worked, was there. About an hour later they sent me a message to come to a certain place on the street, saying they had something for me. After my work was done I went to the designated place and met three men, the two I had met before and a third one, who was Emil Chaillet. I met him then for the first time. This was about the middle of July, 1908. I was then just 17 years old. They took me to a café and treated me, after which we all went to the hotel where Chaillet lived, and the two men whom I met first left me with Chaillet. He induced me to accompany him to the hotel, promising to marry me and to make me very happy. He told me to write to the folks that I had gone away from Paris for fear they might look for me. I never saw the two men that I met first after that, and I never learned their names. Emil Chaillet told me that he never knew them—they never used their right names among themselves. He induced me to go with him and stay with him, promising to make me very happy, as I said before. I asked him how he would make me so happy, and he told me he would marry me, so I went with him to the hotel and stayed with him ever since. I was not even allowed to go back for my clothes or let anyone know where I was.

At first he treated me very kindly for about a month while I lived with him; then he told me he would put me in a place where I could make plenty of money, but did not say how. He told me that we were going to America, but I did not know where. We left Paris during the first days of September, 1908, arriving at Montreal September 21. I traveled with him as his wife, but what name I had as a married woman I do not remember; he gave so many different names I don't believe I could remember all of them. He gave Beretzi at most places, but not at Liverpool. We traveled second class, as man and wife. He would not allow me to speak to anybody. We passed the immigration officers at Quebec as man and wife, but I did not know what name he used; they asked me my maiden name; I gave Pimet, and that I came from Switzerland.

The first time he told me about the kind of business I was to do was on the boat from Liverpool, but I was so young—I was only 17—I did not understand what it meant. He explained all about it; how they lived in houses of prostitution; but I had no idea about what it really meant, even after his explanation. I was helpless. I could not tell my misfortune to anybody. I was afraid he might do me some harm.

When we arrived at Montreal we stayed there one day and then he placed me in a house of prostitution, where I went under the name of ———— ————. I stayed there seven months. Emil Beretzi, as he calls himself, lived at ————. I used to do business there, also. Then he had another place at ————, and I had to go to his place after I was through with business and he compelled me to give him every cent of my earnings—my shameful earnings—which I had to do, as I was very much afraid of him. He once blackened my eyes in Montreal because I went to the theater with another girl and did not practice prostitution. He was not satisfied with the money I made practicing prostitution, but forced me to become a street walker. While doing this I was arrested by the Montreal police and put in jail one month, which was in March, 1909. It was because Beretzi was afraid that both he and I would be arrested if I continued to practice prostitution in Montreal that he took me to Alaska.

We left Montreal on the 17th or 18th of April, 1909. Upon arrival at Vancouver, British Columbia, he put me in a house, the third door from the corner; I don't know the number; it was not far from the wharf. I was sick then—I had an abscess on my neck—and he could not compel me to do any business because my neck was swollen. From there we left for Port Essington, British Columbia. From there we went in a small boat to Prince Rupert, where we stayed one day. From there we took the *City of Seattle* for Skagway, and from there to Fairbanks, Alaska.

When we arrived at Fairbanks we were met by a man named Edward Jalabert, who told us that some women told the immigration officers about us and that we were liable to be arrested, and advised us to go away. We all went to Fifth avenue, to Edward Jalabert's place, where two men came. One was Gus Bovard, an elderly man with grayish hair, whom Beretzi knew a long time ago. Gus traveled with Beretzi together to China and to Russia. We stopped at the Pioneer Hotel only one night, and he took me the next morning on the boat to Tanana, he fearing arrest. He told me he was taking me to Seattle to practice prostitution, as the exposition was on there and that I could make as much money there as in Fairbanks by prostitution.

While we were together at Fairbanks with the three other men, who also lived off the earnings of fallen women, there was a discussion as to what they should do with me—whether to put me in a crib to practice prostitution or not—and finally decided, as I told you, to take me to Seattle. We arrived at Tacoma—I don't remember the date—and had to wait there for some time for a boat, and we were arrested at Tacoma. I believe it was July 3, 1909, and from there you know what happened.

I am very anxious to return to my father and mother and my sisters. I shall never return to this terrible life again. This man, Emil Chaillet, or Beretzi, or, as he called himself in Vancouver, Auberson, or whatever his name is, actually kidnaped me. I had no idea what awaited me. The men who first met me actually sold me to Chaillet, as he later told me himself that he gave them some money for bringing me to him.

I make this truthful statement in every particular, with the understanding that my poor father and mother would not be informed of my misfortune, disgrace, and downfall, and I beg you to send me home and not to tell them anything about me. They are old, and it would break their hearts to know this.

Emil Chaillet asked me to have my little sister, who is 15 now, to come to him, and that he would put her in the same horrible life he did me, but I protested and would not consent to it.

Since Chaillet put me in a house of prostitution at Montreal I have earned more than $2,000, but he kept all that money; he forced me to give the money to him.

Q. On what steamer did you arrive in Canada, at what port, and from what country?

REPORT ON HARBORING WOMEN FOR IMMORAL PURPOSES.

A. I arrived in Canada September 21, 1908, in Montreal, with Beretzi, as his wife; I think it was the steamer Manitoba, from Liverpool.

Q. When did you leave Montreal?

A. About April, 1909; then came to Vancouver, British Columbia; stayed there about three months, and from there came to Ketchikan and Skagway and Fairbanks, Alaska.

Q. What were you doing in Montreal?

A. Practicing prostitution all the time.

Q. Do you wish to make any further statement?

A. No; I have nothing further to state. I have told you the truth in this case.

Q. In accordance with the laws of the United States you may be deported to France, and if you have any reasons to show why you should not be deported, you may do so now.

A. I have no objection to the decision of deportation to France; I want to go back to my father and mother, sisters and brothers, but I do not wish to let them know the life I have been leading here.

APPENDIX IV–1A.

[Letters.]

APRIL 20.

Mr. —— ——:

I am glad to hear good news of your family; my family is well.

Even tho I learn details of your letter, it is, as you know, very difficult to send a woman. If you pay enough money, surely I can carry out the work well. At present, as you know, my social position is quite high, so I can not get a woman myself for you. But you may set your mind at ease about it, because I will request another person to get a woman for you, and then I will be her guardian. If carried out well, the market price of a woman is about $500 at present. At any rate, I request you to pay me about $300 in advance. To tell the truth, I was requested to send some woman by a friend of mine. So on December, 39th year of Meiji (1906), I sent a woman. But he hasn't paid me the whole sum of money yet. Therefore, as soon as you receive this letter then please send me the money. Please, you must send money to Yokohama in my name because I have many friends (the officers of the post-office), but I surely am responsible for this matter. And at the same time please use Mr. ——'s name as a remitter (applicant). Please inform me of their address—what ken, address, and name. I have not yet met the women, so please recommend me to them.

I send compliments,

—— ——.

JULY 1.

Mr. —— ——:

I am glad to hear that your family is well, and my family is well.

Yesterday I received a postal money order of 200 yen and 2 yen and 1 sen from Mr. —— ——, in Yokasuka. So you may set your mind at ease about it.

Please allow me to ask Mr. —— in Yokohama about granting passports as fast as he can, and at the same time even if I applied for the passports, it takes two months or sometimes four months to get them, but as soon as I receive them I will inform you.

If it would be convenient, I may request to send the women secretly by merchant vessel to the vicinity of San Francisco. If I am successful, I will telegraph to you from the landing place, so please do you with money go out to meet them, and you must hear from them about the details of how to land them.

With my compliments,

——.

AFFIDAVIT.

STATE OF WASHINGTON, *County of King, ss:*

—— ——, being first duly sworn on oath, say that I came from Japan Meiji 37 (1904) to San Francisco, Cal., with my cousin and her husband. I came under the name of —— ——. —— ——, the husband of my cousin, requested me to tell the immigration inspectors that my name is —— ——. The passport read also —— ——. I don't know how it was made that way, because he (—— ——) made all the arrangements to get the passport, etc. He told me that I was to be a waitress when I get to this side.

When I landed in San Francisco I was thrown in a room in Chinatown (a place called Cho Clarlie); then I was forced to become a prostitute in a Chinese house of prostitution above named, and continued to practice prostitution till the time of the earthquake of San Francisco.

I came from there to Astoria, Oreg., the same year, in June, and stayed there till November, and then to Portland, Oreg., staying there till March of following year. I came to Bellingham, Wash., and stayed there till September.

—— ——, who is said to be in Vancouver, British Columbia, accompanied or brought me to Bellingham from San Francisco. He demanded $500, saying that he was going to Japan, but in reality went to Canada. Then —— —— acted as my master after —— left me.

Mr. ——, who conducts a house of ill repute in Bellingham, brought me to Seattle. Then I practiced prostitution in Washington house (a house of prostitution on Fifth avenue, South Seattle). I worked there a year and paid $500 to ——, the money I borrowed to pay ——. —— ——, who was with me in Bellingham, borrowed money, a sum in the neighborhood of $800, from ——. I paid this debt of ——, all except the sum of $350, for him. I left him, although he did resist me, but finally he let me go with the understanding that I pay his debts of $700. He got altogether about $800 in cash from me, besides the debts that I paid.

Then —— ——, a married man living in Tacoma, Wash., told me to marry him. First I consented, but in fact I didn't like him, because he was a married man, a gambler, and I knew that if I lived with him I had to lead a life of shame.

I ran away from Tacoma to Everett, and I asked —— of that place to straighten this matter between —— and myself. He told me to go to Seattle, and then he would come down and fix the matter. I came to Seattle, and stayed at the —— Hotel at ——.

Before I went to Tacoma, I went to Miss —— home, who is in charge of —— in city of Seattle. After staying there a couple of days I came downtown to do some shopping. I was caught by the men of ——, owner of the —— House, a place of ill repute in Tacoma, who were searching for me here, and I was taken to Tacoma. —— was waiting for me there and told me to go to do some business at sawmill camps on the Tacoma Eastern Railway, but I refused to obey his orders, and he was very much disappointed. I ran away from the —— Hotel, ——, in Tacoma, and secreted at a friend's home for three days; then I went to Everett to see Mr. ——, as above stated.

On the night of November 22, 1909, Mr. —— came to my room at —— Hotel and struck me on the head as soon as he entered, and he made a pretense of pulling a gun out of his pocket. I saw the revolver in his hand, partly out of his pocket; then I thought he was going to shoot me, because he mentioned that he had a revolver. —— told me to go to Tacoma again but I refused. Then he demanded to pay about $300 cash to ——. This also I refused; as I didn't have the money, and I would have refused even if I had the money.

There were several ruffians who are working under —— instructions and directions outside the hotel (——); —— walked out of the room and called in ——, who was in the hall of the hotel, and came into my room, and —— told —— to watch me, and he answered that he would and told —— to go any place he wanted to. ——, before he left, told —— to watch me well till morning and then he will send another man to relieve him.

During —— absence from my room —— followed me even when I went to the toilet.

A man who happened to see —— strike me went to call a police; —— escaped, but —— was arrested.

I practiced prostitution four years and a half; after all this time I am penniless. As I am not strong, I did not make much. * * * The money I took in, I was instructed by my masters to put in the bank. I paid all my board myself.

——, the man who went to Astoria, Portland, and Bellingham, took every cent I earned, and whenever I refused to give him, he threatened to kill me with a revolver, so I had to give him all the earnings.

I am now seeking protection, and trying to escape from this slavery, for if I am not taken care of, I will be compelled to go back and lead the life of a prostitute, or I might be killed by this gang; I want to be decent and respectable, and will work honestly to earn my living, so please help me.

————— ————.

Subscribed and sworn to before me this 4th day of December, 1909.
[SEAL.]
————— ————,

Notary Public in and for the State of Washington.

(Residing at Seattle, King County.)

REPORT ON HARBORING WOMEN FOR IMMORAL PURPOSES.

Appendix IV.—A.

LETTER TO MEMBER OF IMMIGRATION COMMISSION.

Sir: In pursuance of your request that I inform you of the manifest addresses of certain aliens who, to my knowledge, went to the French Procurers' Club, at 124 West Twenty-ninth street, I beg to submit the following:

Previous to September, 1907, men and women were openly manifested to that address. Since the middle of that month, when the house came under the surveillance of the immigration authorities, such manifestings have wholly ceased. Even before that date some persons intending that as their destination gave false addresses on board ship.

1. Ernest Deville, *La Savoie*, July 21, 1907, second-class passenger, manifested to 116 West Twenty-sixth street. His baggage, check numbers 45, 30, 56, went to 124 West Twenty-ninth street. Auguste, then proprietor of the place, signed for them.

2, 3. Jean and Marie Thomerieux, *La Bretagne*, September 23, 1907, second class, manifested to Hotel Lafayette. Four pieces of baggage went to 124 West Twenty-ninth street for them.

4. Claire Windeliuex, same boat and date, second class, was manifested to Chicago, and also to "brother-in-law, in Hotel Lafayette, New York." Testimony in deportation proceedings later proved that she went to 124 West Twenty-ninth street, although books of express company delivering baggage from that boat did not show it.

5. Maria Jewince, *La Touraine*, October 12, 1907, second class, manifested to 129 West Fortieth. Baggage Nos. 3244 and 3489 went to 129 West Twenty-ninth street.

7. Books of Erie Express Company show that on September 9, 1907, baggage went to 129 West Twenty-ninth street from steamship *La Gascogne*, to a name illegibly written but apparently Damsol or Damisol. This apparently refers to Constant and Josephine Denisot, arrivals by that ship on same date, second class, manifested to Hotel Griffon, New York.

8. Books of Erie Express Company show that on September 28, 1907, two pieces of baggage were delivered from steamship *La Savoie* to Duther or Druthen, 124 West Twenty-ninth street. No such name is on the manifest, showing that the passenger landed under another name entirely.

9, 10. Books of Erie Express Company show that on August 20, 1907, two pieces of baggage were delivered from steamship *La Touraine* to 124 West Twenty-ninth street, to "Claessons," for which Auguste signed. No such name is on manifest. The books show a second lot of baggage from same ship to same address; no name given.

11, 12. Jules and Silvie Carriere, *La Gascogne*, September 9, 1907. Second-class passengers, manifested to Hotel Lafayette. I do not know if they went direct to 124 West Twenty-ninth street, but within a month they received mail there.

13. Leone Supper, *La Gascogne*, November 4, 1907, second class, manifested to husband, Edouard, cook, Hotel Lafayette. Erie Express Company's books show E. Suppin or Suffin (illegible), going, same ship and date, to 124 West Twenty-ninth street. Auguste signed for baggage.

14, 15. Albert Lefebvre and wife, Adrienne, steamship *La Touraine*, November 16, 1907, second class, manifested to Spokane, Wash. Five pieces of baggage went in their name to 124 West Twenty-ninth street from the ship.

16. Jeanne Martin, same ship and date, second class, manifested to uncle in Montreal, went direct to 124 West Twenty-ninth street. (Deported.)

17. Books of Erie Express Company show that on same ship and date one piece of baggage was delivered to 124 West Twenty-ninth street for "P. Lambrick." No such name appears on manifest.

18, 19. Gaston Tardieu and wife, Marie Eulalie, same ship and date, manifested to Hotel Lafayette. Baggage went to 124 West Twenty-ninth street, where they also received mail.

20. Books of Erie Express Company show baggage delivered from *La Larraine*, February 8, 1908, to 134 West Twenty-ninth street for "Cheirre." Armand (then proprietor) signed for it. No "Cheirre" on manifest.

21. Henri Volation, *La Savoie*, April 25, 1908, second class, manifested to Portland, Oreg. Baggage went to 124 West Twenty-ninth street.

22, 23. Charles Fillette and wife, Lucile, steamship *La Provence*, May 30, 1908, entered as citizens; no address given. Three pieces of baggage went in their name to 124 West Twenty-ninth street.

24, 25. Henri Doudelex and wife, Germaine, same ship and dates. Manifested to Hotel Lafayette. Four pieces of baggage went in their name to 124 West Twenty-ninth street.

REPORT ON HARBORING WOMEN FOR IMMORAL PURPOSES.

APPENDIX IV–B.

AFFIDAVITS FROM REPORT OF COMMISSIONER OF POLICE, NEW YORK.

STATE OF NEW YORK,
City and County of New York, ss:

John Doe, being duly sworn, deposes and says: I am a detective in the police department of the city of New York, attached to the detective bureau, Borough of Manhattan, and engaged in getting evidence against alien prostitutes and criminals.

On June 23, 1908, I arrested an alien woman, named Mary Doe, on a warrant issued by the Department of Commerce and Labor, Washington, D. C.

The said Mary was charged with violation of the immigration law (act of Congress, Feb. 20, 1908). She was found guilty and ordered deported by the Department of Commerce and Labor.

In the meantime the United States grand jury in the southern district of New York found an indictment against a man named —— of —— street, New York City, for harboring several prostitutes. The said Mary Doe was therefore held as a witness in this case at the request of the United States attorney.

After the lapse of several months a native-born American citizen by the name of Richard Roe made an application to marry the said Mary Doe. The said application was granted by the Department of Commerce and Labor.

On November 5, 1908, the said Richard Roe (who was at that time divorced from his first wife, under her own application, as the divorce papers show plainly that he was caught in the act of committing adultery with another woman) married the said Mary Doe, who was discharged by the Department of Commerce and Labor, and took her to his house at —— street.

Several days after I met the said Mary Doe, who told me the following:

"Don't you know what he wanted from me, that fellow Roe? Don't you know that he had another girl in his house at —— street, and when we got there he introduced me to her (an old prostitute named Laura) and told me she was his wife, but that I would stay with them and that we both would make good money by both hustling from his house? I therefore left him and went back to —— at —— street, where I have been living a few days. I sent a letter to him stating that I was going to sue him if he didn't give me some money, as I was penniless. He then advised me to return to his house at —— street, and 'do business' there for myself (meaning prostitution). This I did, and I now make $5 or $6 a day, which I keep for myself, and Roe stays with his affinity, Laura."

"Of course you know, John, that if I married that fellow Roe, it was only to beat deportation and be safe forever, as I am now an American citizen."

Since that time I have seen the said Mary Doe, now Mrs. Roe, soliciting on Twenty-sixth street and Sixth avenue and taking men to —— street.

JOHN DOE.

Subscribed and sworn to before me this 23d day of December, 1908.

—— ——,
Commissioner of Deeds.

STATE OF NEW YORK,
City and County of New York, ss:

John Doe, being duly sworn, deposes and says:

I am an officer in the police department of the city of New York, attached to the detective bureau, Borough of Manhattan, and engaged in getting evidence against alien prostitutes and criminals.

On May 19, 1908, there arrived by the steamer *Mauretania* an alien woman named Jane Doe, who was arrested on a warrant issued by the Department of Commerce and Labor, which warrant was obtained by the police department on an affidavit made and sworn to by me. She was ordered deported by the Department of Commerce and Labor on September 2, 1908, and held as a witness in a case now pending.

I met the said Jane Doe on Broadway and Twenty-eighth street during the first part of November, 1908. She came to me, saying:

"Hello; how are you? You didn't expect to see me back in New York, did you? Well, I am going to tell you the whole thing.

"An immigration official down on Ellis Island got 'dead stuck' on me, because I appeared to be a nice girl when I was down there. I know how to behave, when necessary. This man hired a lawyer for me, who got me out of there on a writ of habeas corpus. Some immigration officials got 'wise' to the attention that he was paying me, and he was immediately transferred to Texas. But he came to New York a week ago, and he married me in New Jersey. Here is my marriage certificate (handing same to me), but he (her husband) is now back in Texas, and he wants me to go there, but I won't. I couldn't live with that man; he isn't making enough money. I don't want to go into the dressmaking business and earn $8 or $9 a week when I can make that every day on Broadway. I wish my husband would remain in Texas steady, and I would be all right in New York."

I read the marriage certificate above referred to, which showed that a certain William Doe married Jane Doe in Hoboken, N. J., on October 28, 1908.

Almost every night I see the said Jane Doe (now Mrs. Doe) soliciting on Broadway and taking men to hotels in that vicinity.

JOHN DOE.

Subscribed and sworn to before me this 23d day of December, 1908.

———— ————,
Commissioner of Deeds.

APPENDIX IV-C.

In May, 1908, a French girl of 25 years came to the United States with another girl and a man. She was detained at Ellis Island for inquiry. Her testimony was much confused. In one place she said she was traveling alone, in another that she came with a man and woman, and in still another that she gave money to the man to pay her passage here. She gave her place of destination as a French hotel. When told she could not go there, she asked to be sent to the Sisters of Charity of the French Immigrant Home. She denied that she knew anybody at the French hotel, saying she got the address from a woman in Paris. One of the sisters of the French Home appeared before the board of inquiry and stated that she had talked to the girl and believed her to be of good character. The girl was then discharged. Very shortly thereafter she was arrested and convicted of soliciting in the streets.

Another case is that of Fernand B————. It was positively known that a woman called "Susan" and he arrived in the United States in October, 1807, and that they came on a French steamer. Careful inspection of the manifests failed, however, to reveal their names. Later, when the couple were arrested in Chicago, one of their trunks was seized. On it was pasted a customs label giving the date of its arrival and the name of the ship; yet an inspection of the manifest of that date failed to disclose the name B————. Correspondence found in the trunk was under the names of B———— and B————, but even the latter name was not on the manifest. Another trunk which had been placed in the hold of the French steamer was found later with its baggage label, which was numbered. The number was looked up in a baggage manifest found at the dock where the steamer landed. Through this means it was discovered that Bocquet and the woman "Susan" came over under the name of Fournait. The inspection of a third trunk, found still later, disclosed some letters which bore this last name. It was said at the dock that these baggage manifests were not filed in America, and that it was by accident that this one had not been returned to France.

The agents of this commission attempted to trace the movements after their arrival in the United States of a number of alien women and girls. The following are typical cases:

Three Greek girls were, when entering, booked to a certain address in New York City. The number was that of a little oyster house, with vacant rooms above and no one in charge but a waiter. When this waiter was asked for the man to whom these girls were booked, he said the man did not belong there, but came once in a while and sometimes received his mail there. He said he could give the man's right address and handed the agent the address of a rooming house in the heart of the "Tenderloin"— a place filled with French prostitutes and single Greek men. A French girl of 18 years of age, imported last winter, was recently found there.

Another man brought a woman and was booked to a well-known boarding house in New York City where many pimps and their women stop over night. Upon inquiry at this house a few days later the only address of this couple that could be obtained was that of the French headquarters in Chicago.

A French girl landed in company with a man alleged to be her husband and was detained at the request of one of the immigration inspectors. The girl had every appearance of being a prostitute. Both the girl and the man were booked to Chicago to a man who kept a laun..lry, and who acted as interpreter and business assistant to the French pimps in Chicago. The girl was allowed to land, and two months later was found in a disorderly house in Chicago when it was raided.

Appendix IV–D.

THE GIUSEPPINA PASQUALINA CASE.

The following letter was seized in a raid in New York City.

[Translation.]

MARSEILLE, *May 10, 1908.*

VERY DEAR FRIEND: I had learned from my friend Baptistin that you had sent him a ticket to have a woman sent you. It happens at the moment that this woman has failed, and as I had a woman I was trying to place somewhere and whom I had under my protection, and knowing that Baptistin needed one, I talked to her and I decided to send her to you. Now, dear friend, as I knew that the woman was going to you, I dressed her without regard to expense, for I knew that with you I had nothing to lose; also I was forced to feed her during fifty days. Only I send her to you with all confidence, for the woman is young and very pretty, and is one of our own country-women and easy to train, and you must know that you said in your letter to B. how the woman ought to behave. I gave her the story as you gave it. At her arrival take means to make good offers, for the woman has never traveled and might take it in bad part. Now, dear friend, we have still another woman in view who will do your busi-ness well if you wish; only you know very well there are many difficulties, and espe-cially many expenses. Moreover, you know better than I how that is. Then B. has taken a great deal of trouble and it will be necessary to pay him well, for he deserved it.

Now, dear friend, I have been obliged to dress her from head to foot, and even to give her some pennies to get her off, for without that she would not have gone will-ingly. I bought her a straw hat with cream-colored roses, white silk waist, a marine-blue skirt, a rose-colored scarf, a pair of shoes with black buttons; furthermore, 3 pairs of gloves. All this will serve you as information when she reaches New York. She is a pretty little brunette, with a graceful figure. I have written for her upon a piece of paper the name of the person to whom she is going—her uncle, Solario. Besides that, she can easily take care of herself. She sailed by the steamer *Venezia*, of the Fabre Line.

Let me tell you also that she has had a medical examination; that her health is good. I will not write you anything more, except to ask for a prompt answer and to inform me as to whether you have need of a woman.

I conclude by shaking hands with you heartily.

Thy friend forevermore,

NAPOLEON FARIGO.

With compliments of Baptistin and my wife, I send best regards to your brother and to your wife.

The information contained in this letter was brought to the attention of the commis-sioner of immigration at Ellis Island by this commission, and when the girl mentioned therein arrived she was detained for inquiry. The testimony which is set out below was given by the girl and her uncle before the board of special inquiry. The girl was allowed to land without further inquiry.

[Special inquiry held at Ellis Island, N. Y., May 29, 1908.]

Present: Messrs. Parbury (chairman), Conserve, and Toner, inspectors; Peter Gil-man, secretary; interpreter, Thomasian.

Case of Pasqualina, Giuseppina, 27f; French; steamship *Venezia*, May 28, 1908.

S. L., Inspector Schwartz. L. P. C., Inspector Alexander.

Alien, sworn and examined by Inspector Parbury, testified:

Giuseppina Pasqualina, 27; traveling alone; born in France; single; can not read or write; arrived on *Venezia;* my uncle, Pacifico Solario, paid my passage; domestic; never here before; going to my uncle; I have no money; I have telegraphed to call.

By Mr. TONER:

Q. How long is your uncle in the United States?
A. Seven or eight years. There are two. One of them is married; the other is not. I am going to the married one. His wife is with him. He has no children.
Q. What is your other uncle's name?
A. I am not acquainted with him very well, and they gave me no address, and that is all I know about it.
Q. Who gave you the address at home?
A. My sister in France.

S. Doc. 196, 61–2——4

95

Q. What is your sister's name?
A. Launcette Pasqualina.
Q. Has she ever been in this country?
A. No.

By Mr. PARBURY:

Q. Is your sister married?
A. Yes.
Q. Then her name is not Launcette Pasqualina. What is her husband's name?
A. Louis Pasquine.
Q. What is your purpose in coming to this country?
A. Because my uncle asked me to come.
Q. What do you intend to do here to support yourself?
A. I am going to stay with uncle and work.
Q. How is he your uncle?
A. He is my father's brother.
Q. How is it you and your uncle have not the same name?
A. I don't know; what do you want me to tell you?
Q. How do you explain, your name being Pasqualina and his name Solario, he being a brother of your father?
A. I don't know.
Q. Why did you say he is your father's brother if you do not know?
A. He is my father's brother; I would not be here if I had not confidence in him.
Q. What is your father's name?
A. Francis.
Q. And your mother's?
A. Maria; she is dead.
Q. Has your father any brothers other than the one you mention?
A. No.
Q. Any sisters?
A. No.
Q. Is your father alive?
A. Yes.
Q. Where?
A. In Ajaccio.
Q. Do you speak Italian?
A. Yes.
Q. Was your father an Italian?
A. No.
Q. Is it your uncle to whom you are going?
A. No.
Witness, sworn and examined by Inspector PARBURY, testified:
Q. What is your name?
A. Pacifico Solario.
Q. Where do you live?
A. 61 Mott street.
(Interpreter Thomasian here said that the witness was speaking in Italian and he did not feel fully competent to interpret. Interpreter Frabislis succeeded him.)
(Examination resumed.)
Q. Who do you call for here?
A. I call for Pasqualina Guseppina; she is a relative of my wife.
Q. How long have you been in the United States?
A. Fifteen years.
Q. Are you a citizen?
A. Yes.
Q. Final papers?
A. Yes.
Q. Where is your wife?
A. In Mott street with me; I have four children; one 14 years old, one 9 years old, one 8 years old, and one 14 months.
Q. How are you employed?
A. I have a stand on the street.
Q. What is your income from that business?
A. Ten dollars to $12 a week.
Q. Have you saved any money?
A. Yes. (Shows bank book on C. Russo & Co., 93 Mulberry street, New York, in which is deposited $60 in favor of his daughter Lucia Rosina Solario.)
Q. What was your wife's maiden name?

A. Josephine Ferrara.
Q. Is she an Italian?
A. Italian, born in Marseille, France.
Q. Where were you born?
A. In Italy.
Q. How long is your wife in this country?
A. Twelve years.
Q. Has the girl any relative here aside from your wife?
A. No; only my wife.
Q. Did you pay her passage?
A. Yes.
Q. Why?
A. My wife is sick and I preferred to have some one related to her take care of her.
Q. How many rooms have you?
A. Four rooms.
Q. Is your wife in bed?
A. Yes, she is sick; she will soon have a baby.
(Alien recalled.)
Q. Do you know this man?
A. I know him; he is my uncle.
Q. What is his name?
A. I do not remember the name.
Q. Do you know his wife?
A. No; I don't know his wife.
Q. Do you know anyone in this country by the name of Josephine Ferrara?
A. Yes; I know she is his wife.
Q. Is she related to you?
A. Yes.
Q. Why don't you tell the truth?
A. It is the truth; I was so young when they left.
Q. Have you sisters or brothers here?
A. No; I have no relative in the United States besides these two.
(To the witness:)
Q. Have you any brothers or sisters in the United States?
A. No.
Q. Has your wife?
A. No.
Q. Do you know whether or not this girl has any relatives here aside from you and your wife?
A. No.

By Mr. TONER:

Q. Did you ever live at 93 Mulberry street?
A. That is where I get my letters.
Mr. TONER. I move to defer, pending the appearance of wife of witness before this board.
Mr. CONVERSE. I second the motion.
Mr. PARBURY. Deferred.

[Second board. At a special inquiry held at Ellis Island, June 2, 1908.]

Present: Messrs. Parbury (chairman), Toner, and Converse, inspectors. Convened at 9.30 a. m. Schwarting, stenographer; Mr. Rothe, interpreter.
Deferred case of Pasqualina, Giuseppina, 26f; French; ex steamship *Venezia*, May 28, 1908.
Witness, sworn and examined by Inspector Parbury, testified:
My name is Pacifico Salario.
Q. What is your address?
A. Sixty-one Mott street, New York.
Q. You appeared before this board yesterday, did you not?
A. Yes.
Q. And we suggested that you send your wife down here. Where is she?
A. My wife could not come, so I got a certificate from the doctor, stating that she could not come.

" *To whom it may concern:*

"This certifies that Mrs. Josephine Pacifico Solario, living at 61 Mott street, is in the last stages of pregnancy; she had very hard sufferings in the last couple of months on account of weak heart—fatty infiltration of the heart—from which she is unable to ride on carriage, train, or car, and unable to walk for long way.

"Per faith, June 1, 1908.

"Dr. G. Di Santi.

"Giuseppe Russo, *Notary*."

Q. What additional have you to say this morning from what you said on the previous hearing?

A. I have nothing else to say.

Q. If she is permitted to land, where will she stay?

A. First, she can assist my wife, and then if she wants to marry—I won't let her get out of my house until she is married.

Q. She is to live in your house and care for your wife; is that the idea?

A. Yes; my wife is always sickly, and she can help my wife a great deal.

Q. If she should desire to return, you would pay her passage?

A. Yes; I will pay her passage back from here.

Mr. Toner. I move to admit.

Mr. Converse. I second the motion.

Mr. Parbury. Admitted.

Appendix V–A.

LETTERS SHOWING WORKINGS OF THE SYSTEM OF EXPLOITATION.

Dear Leon: If you were smart, your place would be here this moment in Chicago. Your former woman has an under mistress who gives her $50 a week, and, according to somebody who is well versed in the matter, says she will soon receive a share from M. Leon. She is a woman who has a Jew for her man, and if you come to Chicago with your woman you might send her to California, and in that way you might have a chance to pay court to this second woman, and it seems to me that it will be a chance for you. Above all, try to reach the place as soon as possible. You can come to Chicago very cheap, and once there your wife will largely make her way at the home of Mrs. Leon. Women nowadays pay with but two checks a day, and they are not in debt; they can buy where they like. As for me, I see that I can make my way there. I don't want to tell you under what name I go at present. I will only give you a glimpse of the future if you will understand. If you do not understand now, you never will.

Hoping soon to have the pleasure of seeing you. When you arrive you can stop at Mother ——, who has some very good rooms. Mrs. —— herself will receive your wife there, and once inside, your entrance is assured. Don't be a fool, and listen to good advice.

True Friend.

Dear Camille: I have it from reliable sources that the immigration government and the government officials and the Secret Service are after me, and try their best to get evidence against me. I hope they will find none. * * *

—— was pinched yesterday in Omaha with one named ——; it is R— who had sent her there. She was with J. P——, who himself had trouble with this woman.

For ——, the former woman of L. P——, I called for her yesterday; she came with a Jew, who is her man. I don't think he counts for anything in the case. She wants her jewelry back or she will raise a racket. * * * She is headstrong and willing to fight to a finish, but in case of extremity I could get the local police to make her keep quiet.

* * * I sent the man over the road for four years and kept his woman for extra profit. You will admit that the deal is somewhat beastly, and a man would not act that way. * * * She also told me that she has letters in her possession regarding the importation by him to the United States of one certain Rosie and Frette. You will answer me in regard to this, but I believe the best is to blow back. This will simplify matters for him.

Dear Louis: You should have confidence in me, for it is for my good as well as yours. Write me if you have gone with Lea ——, if she is more submissive than before. Dear Louis, when I am there you will not make any difference between me and Lea. It would give me much pain. You have never known how much I think about you, as you have been good to me.

From one pimp to another:
* * * I expect to get pinched any minute. I have things fixed up with the proprietor of the new hotel at which I am living to say that I am employed as elevator boy in case of trouble. I most surely think that my showing my physician's certificate that I am under medical treatment—and my employer will go in front of me—so you see I am pretty well fixed for the present. I am also inclosing in this letter clipping of this morning's paper so you can read for yourself how bad things look in this city for boys ever since the newly appointed mayor took office last Monday. He means business. * * *

From a girl to her mother:
DEAR MOTHER: I am worried because I want to send you something, but you know that I do not know English. I can not go to the post-office. My mistress is always sick. I think she will go to the post-office this week for me. Anyhow, do not worry about it. I will send you what I promised every month. Tell me if you have written to me in New York, because it would be funny if I did not get it.
Apparently letters to this girl remained undelivered, while her letters to her mother were never posted.
While the above letter was found in Chicago, a number of letters from the mother of this girl addressed to her in New York were found at the French Club in New York unopened and undelivered.
The following anonymous letter was received by Judge Landis in Chicago on July 11, 1908:

JULY 10, 1908.

JUDGE LANDIS: Yesterday I went to a sporting house at ——— street and heard a little story which I think I am in duty bound to explain. Eight months ago the madam of the house, Mrs. ——— ———, went to Italy. There she met a nice young lady and told her she is worth a lot of money and other things and finally gets the girl to come to America. When she arrived in Chicago she was brought to her own house, ——— street, and told the truth and that she will have to be a sporty girl. She finally makes the girl make up her mind and everything goes all right, she turning every cent she made to the landlady. A friend of the landlady's came round and the landlady sold her to this man. Things went around until the landlady saw she was losing money on the bargain and wanted the girl back. She could not get her. The consequence was that this girl was slashed a dozen times or more with a razor on the back and face, disfiguring her for life. After being cured at the hospital, Cook County, she went direct to ——— street. The landlady can not make money with a disfigured girl, so to get rid of her she is going to send her out West this week. She also had another girl to whom she is doing the same and who is an American girl 17 years old. On account of the recent raids on the South Side she has this girl hid at No. — ——— street. The first girl went to Harrison Street Station, but everything was fixed up O. K. Her name is ——— ———.

APPENDIX V–B.

[From statement by United States District Attorney Sims.]

A very few days ago this pitiful case was, in an official way, brought to my attention: A little German girl in Buffalo married a man who deserted her about the time her child was born. Her baby is now about 8 or 9 months old. Almost immediately after her husband ran away she formed the acquaintance of an engaging young man who claimed to take a deep interest in her welfare, and in that of a certain girl friend of hers. He persuaded them both that if they would accompany him to Chicago he would immediately place them in employment which would be far more profitable than anything they could obtain in Buffalo. Supposing that the work awaiting her was entirely legitimate and respectable, the little mother took her baby and, in company with the young man and her friend came to Chicago. The next task of this human fiend was to persuade this "child widow" that it would be necessary for her to place her baby temporarily in a foundling's home, in order that it might not interfere with her employment. This accomplished, he took the two young women at once to a notorious house and sold them into white slavery. Thenceforth this fellow has lived in luxury upon the shameful earnings of these two victims. The young mother has attempted by every means imaginable to escape from his clutches and at last has importuned him into a promise to release his hold upon her on the payment of $300. She is still "working out" the price of her release. It is scarcely too much to say that she looks twice her age.

A girl of 18 came to this country in January, trusting to the promise of a woman procurer to give her honest work. She was placed immediately in a house of prostitution and was told that she must earn the cost of importing her before she could be free. She earned the $300 required, and asked the proprietor of the house to free her. He refused to grant her request and she attempted to run away. He followed her to the street and slashed her face so badly that she is now frightfully disfigured. She was pregnant when found by one of the agents of this commission.

An Italian girl who is now serving a term in one of the penal institutions of the State of New York said that while she was an unwilling inmate of an Italian disorderly house in Rochester, N. Y., she overheard a conversation in which a plan to disfigure her face by slashing it was discussed. She escaped and went to the nearest police station and told the captain what had occurred. When the case came up for trial and the man she accused was brought before her she was so frightened that she did not tell the truth, said she was mistaken in the charge, and the case was dismissed. She is afraid to leave the institution. She said to an agent of the commission that these men who disfigured the Italian girls are members of the "Black Hand.'

AFFIDAVIT OF AGENT OF IMMIGRATION COMMISSION.

STATE OF NEW YORK, *County of New York, ss:*

―――― ―――― being duly sworn, deposes and says that he has been for a period of three years last past employed by the United States Government to make special investigations, and as a special agent, and is such at the present time. That during the years 1908 and 1909 he was employed in investigations into the violations of section 3 of the immigration act which has reference to the importation of women into the United States for immoral purposes; that prior to this employment deponent for a period of seven years had been in charge of the criminal department of a private detective agency, and by reason of his connection with investigations into criminal work deponent had become familiar with the restricted districts; had a personal acquaintance with the majority of the proprietors of the disorderly houses and knew many of the inmates of the houses; that his attention was first called to the violations of section 3 of the immigration act by the appearance of immigrant women, inmates of the restricted district, whose faces were unfamiliar, and from whose general appearance and actions deponent felt sure had only been in the United States a short time.

That during his employment as such special agent investigating into the violations of section 3 of the immigration act deponent has secured evidence of such violations in 68 cases, which cases were in different parts of the United States—some in Washington, Idaho, Oregon, and in Alaska. Some of these cases were in violation of the part of section 3 of the immigration act which prohibited harboring; some were in violation of that part of section 3 prohibiting importing; and others were against immigrant women practicing prostitution in the United States within three years after their entry into the United States.

That during the time when deponent was gathering evidence in these cases and during the prosecutions which followed as a result of the evidence deponent talked with a great many of the immigrant women and with a large number of the procurers and the persons responsible for the bringing in of these girls; that from the immigrant women in the United States in violation of section 3 of the immigration act, their procurers, and others responsible for their being so in the United States deponent learned the stories of their importation, the way in which they were placed into the life of a prostitute, the manner of that life, the amount of money derived from the services of such immigrant women, and, in some cases, the condition of slavery in which the women lived. Some of these stories so told to deponent and which deponent, from his knowledge of social conditions and his personal observations of this work, and from the additional fact that in many instances he was able to verify them by the records at the different ports of entry and by the evidence which came out in the different trials of similar cases, believes to be true, are as follows:

A Japanese girl, aged 16, was brought into the United States via Canada, through Victoria, and taken to Bellingham, Wash., in the spring of 1908. She was sent from Japan as a proxy wife to meet her husband, who was a Japanese laborer in America. The husband was represented at the immigration station by a Japanese interpreter who is known to be a Japanese procurer. At the immigration station the Japanese whose wife she was said to be met her and the couple were married in the presence of the immigration authorities, ―――― vouching for the husband's standing and character. The husband took the wife to Bellingham, Wash., and lived with her for several days in a rooming house which was occupied principally by prostitutes; the husband then left the woman and she was immediately taken charge of by a Japanese woman who managed a house of prostitution near by. At the end of two weeks' time the woman who ran the house of prostitution took the young wife to Seattle and sold her to a proprietor of a disorderly house named ————. The woman in Bellingham attempted to break the girl into the life of a prostitute; the girl refused to enter the life, and the woman beat her and starved her, which treatment continued during the entire time of two weeks. At the end of the two weeks the woman, realizing that she could not manage the girl, took her to Seattle and sold her, as above stated, for $1,600.

————, who bought the girl, made the purchase with the intention of sending the girl to Alaska, and the woman from Bellingham was to deliver the girl on the boat about to leave for Alaska. The $1,600 was to cover all expenses of importing the girl from Japan, the expense of the proxy marriage, including the price paid the Japanese who acted as husband, and all expenses of the delivery of the girl on board the boat for Alaska. The girl was taken to Alaska and placed in a house of prostitution. She rebelled up to the time the boat started and wept and fell upon her knees on the dock, begging not to be sent. The woman from Bellingham, who spoke English, forced the girl onto the boat and then explained to the officers of the boat that the girl was her daughter and did not wish to leave because she had a lover in Bellingham. The truth concerning the entire case was not discovered until after the girl had sailed for Alaska.

Another girl, Polish Jew, aged 17, entered the United States through the Ellis Island port, booked for Montana. The procurer in this case was a Jew, and got this girl near the border of Russia by promises of marriage after they reached the United States. At the immigration station he gave their names as man and wife. He took the girl directly from New York to Montana, and broke her into the life there. He put her in a crib, and forced her to lead the life of a prostitute. They stayed in ———— about six weeks, and he then took her to Seattle, Wash., and put her in the crib house of which ————, a Japanese, is the proprietor, and in which there are Japanese, Jewish, and French women as inmates. He kept her there about a month, and then moved her to the ———— House, a house of prostitution of French and Jewish inmates. At the time he placed her in the ———— House the girl was about two and a half months pregnant. Up to this time she had hoped that the man would marry her. When he found that she was pregnant he refused to marry her, but made her work as an inmate in the house of prostitution daily, and collected all her money; he refused to give her any street clothes, and made her continue to work during her pregnancy and up to the time she went to the hospital. She did not go to the hospital until the day before her child was born. She was forced to continue her work when she was too ill to walk, and suffered terrible pain. The man refused to give her any money, and she went to a charitable hospital. While she was in the hospital, the man took another prostitute and left Washington for Butte, Mont.

Another girl, French, aged 19, was brought by a man from Paris to Seattle via New York. The man who imported her was ————, a well-known French importer and procurer of women, and a man whose chief business is to trade and traffic in girls in the following manner: If a procurer is unable to satisfactorily control his girl, he notifies ————, and ———— advises him to let the girl go, and for a consideration he will immediately get him a girl in her place. ———— then becomes acquainted with the girl and introduces her to another man who is in similar trouble with his girl; that is, a man who has a girl whom he can not satisfactorily control. Before the girls realize it they have exchanged positions and ———— has been paid by both men.

When ———— arrived in Seattle with the girl he sold her to another man, who placed her in crib No. — in ———— crib house in Seattle. She became pregnant and was forced by her owner to continue work for seven months, during which time she was forced to turn over all her earnings to the man. She rebelled, but it did no good, as she was told she must continue to work. Finally, in desperation, she took to robbing her patrons, and in this way a complaint was made against her by a patron to the officer on the beat. This deponent was with the officer at the time, and went with him to arrest the girl. After seeing her condition and hearing her story, no arrest was made. Two days later the girl was taken by another girl to the hospital. The man would not give her a cent of money or aid her in any way. He disappeared from Seattle after learning that the story of the girl's condition had been told to the officers. At the time the officers went to make this arrest it was past midnight; the girl had been working in the crib since 4 o'clock of the afternoon before, and the only money that she had with which to pay her car fare (from their room to her crib) and to buy food was 15 cents, which was all the man would give her. She paid 5 cents car fare and 10 cents for a ham sandwich and two butter cakes.

Another girl, French, aged 15, was working in Paris in a factory. On her way home, one evening, she met a man and woman who spoke to her and asked her into a drinking place to have something warm. She went, and they told her she was unusually pretty and that they had a young man friend whom they would like to have her meet. The next night they met her again and had with them the young man. The young man made love to her and accomplished her ruin—after which she left her parents and never returned to them. The man put her on the streets in Paris. She became pregnant and continued to work as a prostitute until the end of six months' pregnancy. The man took care of her and after her child was born pursuaded her to leave Paris and come to America with some friends of his who were in Paris. She did not want to leave her child, but did so and came to America with these friends. They took her to Chicago and she was there turned over by the ———— to a man who took her to Butte, Mont. She lived with this man in Butte, Mont., for about a year, turning over all of her earnings to him; then she discovered that while she was giving him all her money from her earnings in a crib he was treating parlor-house girls to wine. Violent disagreements then arose between them and she was finally placed in jail for stabbing him. After her time was served she left Butte and went to Seattle, where she has since practiced prostitution, but has at no time given any of her earnings to a man. From her earnings she has been sending money to Paris to care for and educate her child. At the present time she is in ————, ————, where she has two houses of prostitution, one with four inmates and the other with three inmates. She does not practice prostitution herself at the present time.

Sworn to before me this 6th day of November, 1909.

Q. What is your full name?
A. Marie S————.
Q. How old are you?
A. Twenty-five years.
Q. Are you still a German subject?
A. Yes.
Q. Never been married?
A. No.
Q. What occupation did you have in Germany?
A. First I was four years a trained nurse in Germany, then I went to France and was a governess for one year, and after that I came home and assisted running the house.
Q. Where are your parents?
A. In ————, Prussia, and also my four brothers.
Q. When did you first leave Europe for the United States?
A. On the 29th of September this year; I left Bremerhoffen on the steamship *Kaiser Wilhelm II*, on the same day as Marie G————.
Q. Who is this Marie G————?
A. I do not know her except that I became acquainted with her on board the ship; I do not know her parents.
Q. Where were you going when you left Germany?
A. I wanted to go to Rochester, N. Y., in company with my friend, Katie H————, and was a friend of my mother's, and she frequently visited us, and I had the intention of coming to America; and on one of these occasions she told me if I wanted to come with her I could.
Q. Where did you go when you landed in New York?
A. We went to the Hotel ————, in Hoboken.
Q. Who went with you to the ———— Hotel?
A. Marie G————, Mr. Kalt S————, and his brother, and Miss Eliza W————, a girl that Marie G———— brought over with the intention of taking her along with her.
Q. Where did you see Eliza W———— last?
A. Eliza W————'s brother came to the hotel in Hoboken, took her downstairs, had a conversation with her, and probably induced her to go with him, though I was not present at the conversation, because she took her things away and went with her brother. Marie G———— had prepaid her ticket to Seattle, although she told me it was for California; the following day Marie G———— was quite indignant at Eliza's going away, took the ticket away from her, went to the office and had it transferred to my name.
Q. What is the name and address of the brother of Eliza?
A. I do not know; Marie G———— has it.
Q. How did you come to fall in with Marie G————?
A. On my way to Bremerhoffen in the train Marie G———— happened to be in the same compartment. Marie G———— asked whether I was going to America. She asked me all about myself and my family. Had I suspected the nature of her mission I would not have confided anything to her. She told me that she worked very hard around the camps in America as a cook, and also her sister and her husband. The nature of the work that she claimed to have done seemed to me almost impossible

for a woman, but she was so emphatic that I believed her. She told all of us that she had to drive for hours sometimes to get water for the camp where she worked, although I doubted it, but I heard so much that I really did not pay any further attention to it after all. She told me that she was a respectable married woman and owned a house in Los Angeles, Cal., and said that she just made a visit to Germany and was going back to Los Angeles, Cal., to join her husband.

Q. What was the name of this husband that Marie G—— spoke of?

A. She gave her name as Marie G—— at the ticket office on the ship, and I naturally thought her husband's name was G——.

Q. On the ship did Marie G—— ask you to go with her to California?

A. No.

Q. Where did she first extend the invitation to you to accompany her?

A. When we arrived at Hoboken my friend from Rochester, N. Y., Katie H——, took sick, an operation was performed on her at Hoboken, and the doctor advised her to remain there some time before proceeding to her home in Rochester. I was alone, did not know the language, and didn't know what to do, and I am not sure whether Marie G—— asked me to accompany her; but since Marie G—— had told me that she was a respectable married woman, owned a house, and was going to join her husband in Los Angeles, Cal., I thought it quite natural to ask her if she could not assist me in obtaining a position. She willingly consented. She knew I had no money, and as Eliza's brother took Eliza away, she changed that ticket and asked me to come with her to Los Angeles, Cal. I was of the opinion that we were going to Los Angeles, Cal., and did not think that we were going to Seattle, because Marie G—— had led me all the way to believe that we were going to California. I did not know we were going to Seattle until after we landed here. The same day that we arrived in Seattle she mentioned to me that since she was short of money; that we would probably have to stay in Seattle until we had sufficient money to continue the voyage. Marie G—— received $100 in Hoboken and twice on our way West she received $50 each time.

Q. From whom did she get that money?

A. She told me the first $100 came from her sister, and that her sister was well off and married; the second time she told me that she had telegraphed for $50 to a good friend of hers, and how she obtained it the third time I do not know.

Q. When Marie G—— asked you to accompany her, what did you expect to do, what kind of work?

A. I understood either as a nurse, as a governess, or as a domestic.

Q. Did Marie G—— say that she would get you that kind of work?

A. Yes; she said that there was plenty of work and it would be easy here to get a position; she said, "I will be good to you; we will remain together good friends."

Q. When did you reach Seattle?

A. I do not know the exact date, but we were five or six days on the way. In Chicago we remained over night; Marie G—— knew I had no money, and already on the way out she began to treat me rather harshly. The ticket I traveled on was in Eliza W——'s name, and I repeatedly asked her to ask the conductor whether it would be all right, but she always answered me gruffly and said I could stay in Chicago, knowing very well I did not have a cent of my own.

Q. When you reached Seattle with Marie G—— where did you go?

A. We went to a hotel, the name of which I do not know. She told me we will only remain over night. I told her, "How is it we are not going to California? You own a house there." She said to me she had sold the house there in California, and had bought one in Seattle.

Q. How far from the railroad station was the hotel that you and Marie G—— stopped at?

A. Probably ten minutes' walk.

Q. Did you walk up hill or was it on the level?

A. We walked a little on a hill to the right; walked straight up from the station a couple of blocks, and then to the right.

Q. How many nights did you stay at this hotel?

A. Two nights.

Q. Was Marie G—— with you both nights?

A. Yes; I had a room for myself, and Marie with her alleged husband in the other.

Q. Who was this alleged husband?

A. She used to call him Claude; on the ship she did not wear her wedding ring, but when she came here she put it on. I presume she put that ring on in order to make believe that she was married.

Q. Then where did you go?

A. After two nights she told me, "Well, now we go to my house." Of course, I did not know the nature of the house. She told me that she left the house in an uncollected state of affairs, and that she would have to fix it up; I followed her. The house was not far from the hotel; it was a wide shack; it made a very bad impression on me, but still I went in with her; I saw girls half dressed, and Marie turned on me right away, and said I should not bother about what I saw, and not look around so much.

Q. Where was that house?

A. I do not know; it is the same house where the officers got me.

Q. You went into that house when?

A. It was in October, two days after we arrived in Seattle, about the middle of the month.

Q. What did Marie G——— say to you after you were in this house?

A. As soon as I got into the house I saw the girls there. I turned to Marie G——— and wanted to know what they were; she told me not to bother, not to be afraid, that I will easily learn the same thing.

Q. What was this that she spoke of?

A. I presume she meant to become a prostitute.

Q. How long were you in that house where the prostitutes were?

A. About five weeks.

Q. Why did you not leave there?

A. Marie G——— always told me to keep out of sight of the policemen, and I did not know where to go; I had no money; I was alone and did not know what to do; I was afraid to speak to anyone, in fact.

Q. What kind of women were there in this house?

A. They were all French, and Marie G——— would not allow me to speak to any of them. If they were to ask me a question or to speak to me she would always step on my toe as a sign of admonition. One day there were three gentlemen at a table and one of them spoke a little German, but Marie G——— forbade me to speak to them, and all the five weeks I was there she would not allow me to speak to anyone.

Q. What did you do those five weeks?

A. I could not stand it any more; I was there two weeks and I played that I was sick; Marie G——— wanted me to smile and jolly the men, but I could not do it. She put me as a doorkeeper, but at night Marie G——— insisted that I should go with men, so as to pay my expenses.

Q. What was Marie G——— doing?

A. Marie G——— used to tell me that she was clearing from $40 to $50 a day as a prostitute. Almost every minute of the day she would ask me how much I had, so that in case I had any she could take it from me. She took my money away, claiming that she would write it in a book and as soon as I would leave the house she is going to give it to me; but she never gave it to me. She even took my trunk into her room. I asked her repeatedly for my effects in my trunk, and she always asked me if I was afraid she would keep it.

Q. Why did not you leave?

A. I was scared. Marie G——— always scared me with the policemen. She told me that whenever a policeman was near to run away and hide myself, and I thought the penalty was so severe that I did not run away from the house. One day two or three gentlemen came and I believe that they belong to this service. Marie G——— asked me if I spoke to them, and she advised me not to talk to anyone. One of them asked me how business was. I think it was the very same man that arrested us that evening who asked me how business was.

Q. Why didn't you write to your friends?

A. As soon as we arrived at the hotel I asked Marie G——— for some paper. I wanted to write home to my folks; she always kept putting me off; never would give it to me.

Q. Where was this house where the officers found you?

A. The same house—I do not know the street, nor number, or anything. I had no idea where I was. All of the time I was there I was not out of the house at all. I begged Marie G——— once to let me go and look for a position and asked her to accompany me, to show that I really wanted to get a position, but she only laughed at me and asked me if I was crazy and that she could not sacrifice her business.

Q. In all this time you did not know the address?

A. I asked her often for the address. I was crying and she said that she had done so much for me already that I was really ungrateful. I think it was one Sunday I started to cry and threatened to kill myself if she did not let me out, and I told her I was going to get a policeman, and Marie G——— said that if I got a policeman I would get arrested, and not her.

Q. What were you doing all the time you were in the house?

A. For nearly two weeks I did what the others did; in fact, I often sent away men, I was so disgusted. After that I was made a doorkeeper through my repeated entreaties and my telling her that I was sick and could not stand it any more. Maria G——— insisted upon my going with men during the night, but I absolutely refused. She asked me whether I would expect her to keep me for nothing and give me money. Whenever I wanted anything she used to telephone to Claude, and the last Sunday I insisted on getting the address so I could telegraph to my friend in Washington to get $100. When Claude came he asked me what I wanted, and I told him that I wanted a pen and wanted the address of the house, but Claude would not give me the address, and took the address of my cousin in Washington and promised to telegraph for money for me. The next morning I asked Claude whether he had received any money, and he said "No." Claude went on a trip for three or four days. I often asked Marie G—— for the address, which she refused to give me. Although Claude told me he had telegraphed, I received no answer. Since then I have written to my friend to find out if Claude had written, but have as yet received no answer. I am satisfied now that Claude told me a lie and that he did not telegraph.

Q. What is the name and address of your cousin?

A. Clara S——, care A—— C——.

Q. Have you any other relatives in the United States?

A. I have three step-cousins in America, one in New York by the name of ——. I have got a cousin married; her name is now ——, ——. The other one is named Marie. A first cousin, ——, who has a place in ——. I do not know her address. I have another cousin, Clara, in —— also. That is all the relatives I have.

Q. Did you have the intention when you left Germany of entering such a house with Marie G——?

A. No; never entered my mind. I never knew what that kind of a house was, in fact.

Q. Is Marie G—— still in possession of your clothes?

A. No; my trunk is here, but she has some of my things at her house still.

Q. While you were in this house with her did you have possession of your trunk and things, etc.?

A. No. Marie G—— kept my trunk and key in her room, and whenever I wanted anything I was always obliged to go to her. Three days before I was arrested a gentleman who spoke some German visited us and spoke very kindly to me. He asked me how I got into this house and whether I knew the nature of the place. I was so glad to hear him speak German that I begged him to do all he could to take me out of this house; he told me to get my things ready, he was so sure he could take me out, and to be ready by Sunday; I told him the mistress of the house had my things and I could not get them. He told me I should get a policeman. As soon as he went away I went to Marie G—— and insisted upon getting my trunk. After an argument she gave me the trunk but retained the key, and the key is still in her possession. He asked me to give him my name and I gave him my correct name; I did not give him the name that was given me in the house; and he cautioned me not to say anything to anyone and I would be surely taken out of the house. This was about three or four days before I was arrested; the gentleman did not speak to Marie G—— at all, and she did not have any idea that he had spoken to me. Whenever gentlemen came to drink, she made me charge a dollar, and she would always ask me whether I had obtained the money, and as soon as I got it she took it away from me. She would take in as high as $20 in a short time. They charged a dollar for each bottle, and Marie would take in $20 in beer alone in a short time.

Q. Did that gentleman who spoke German to you ever come back?

A. No; he never came back. I was waiting all day Sunday for him. I was in despair. He did not show up, and on Monday we were arrested, and when I was arrested for the minute of course I was frightened, but was at the same time overjoyed to be taken away from the place.

Q. Was that at the time that Marie G—— was arrested?

A. Yes, at the same time, and when the gentlemen came in to ask for Marie G——, Marie G—— pointed to me and said, "There she is," but I immediately said: "No, my name is Marie S——," and he then said, "Yes, I want Marie S——, too." I did not know who the gentlemen were; I merely acted in good faith. Marie G—— closed the door on the gentlemen, and claimed it was all on account of me that she got into trouble. I think that she jumped into the kitchen to get a knife, but one of the gentlemen jumped in after her, and when Marie G—— came to the house here (the detention house), before she was taken upstairs and questioned, she cautioned me not to say anything to the officers, as they would give me a thorough examination, and not to say anything at all about Claude—that I lived with him—and should not even say that I knew Claude; I should not ask any questions, and make them believe I was stupid.

Q. What would you like to do now in this country?

A. I would like to go as a nurse or governess, but I prefer nurse.

Q. How long were you a nurse?

REPORT ON HARBORING WOMEN FOR IMMORAL PURPOSES.

A. Four years in a hospital—in the City Hospital—and then at the clinic of Professor Z——— at Frankfort on the Main.
Q. Did you graduate as a nurse?
A. You get a diploma after seven or eight years, but I got so nervous that I had to give it up for a while. My specialty was in the surgical department and for skin diseases.

Parts of the remainder of the testimony as to her treatment in the house, the demand that she submit to unnatural practices, and such matters are entirely unfit for repetition. In order finally to break her in, Claude V———, with the connivance of Marie G———, his wife, took Marie S——— back to the hotel where they had first stayed, where he, in the cruelest way, committed criminal assault, stifling her efforts to scream by gagging her, until she fainted and was sick for a considerable time afterwards. Both the alien woman and the woman procurer were deported. The man was sentenced to two years' imprisonment for importing the woman passing for his wife. Under the existing national law, which does not hold harboring a crime, he is not liable to any punishment for his unspeakably brutal treatment of his victim.

Appendix VI–A.

LETTERS.

a Omaha, Nebr., *December 9, 1907.*

My Darling Lover: I am immensely bored as well as my lover. We have not had great success since your departure. It is very cold here, but I am not writing you in idle jest, but to speak seriously to you. If this letter reaches you in time, you must answer at once. Business is going from bad to worse. Madam Marion and Madam Alphonse are going to leave Omaha. I would like to take over the crib of Madam Marion, but I do not want to pay $100. In the first place, I have not got them; secondly, if I may not have it with your consent, I will leave as soon as I shall have a little money laid by, either for Butte or Spokane. Answer me at once, for you know I am crazy when I can not earn money.
I hope you had a pleasant trip and it did not tire you.
Awaiting your answer, I embrace you a thousand times, as I love you.
Your darling Madelon, who is lonesome,

Jeanne M. ———.

One word more—answer me at once.

Dear Brother: I feel impressed to write to you these lines to give you tidings of myself, which, by the way, are not very good for the time being. At the present moment I am at Omaha since day before yesterday, and I left with Angele, only she took another route. I will not tell you how she arrived and how she brought the news. ——— made me leave at once for Omaha. The country is prosperous and my wife works out at a sporting house for the present, and as soon as business prospers a little I will try to join you in Helena. I beg you not to let anyone know where I am. There are enough cows to give me away, above all, if the rascal Joli finds out he can fix me. Above all, I beg you to keep silent; tell them if you like I am in Canada, but never say I am in Omaha. If they find out ——— woman I may find myself cut in the throat, as you well know.
As Angele has told me they are trying to find him who brought or sent her to Chicago, you understand better than I do all the hubbub there is. Here I am well fixed for the moment and awaiting developments.
Try and write me as soon as possible and give me all the news about your tribe and also that has happened to Ali's wife and of the concubine that I established in Chicago.
My wife send you her regards. Angele gave me a postal card to mail to you, but I never thought of it again, but that makes no difference, as she had left; she had only time to eat a bite, because she arrived at 5 and she left at 6.30. In case you leave for Helena send your address so I can write at once. Let me repeat, keep absolutely silent; don't tell anybody where I am, for I am always worrying about that.
I will finish, giving you a heartfelt embrace, as well as my wife.
Your affectionate brother,   ——— ———.
Here is my address; write me under that name: Monsieur ——— ——— —— ——— street, Omaha, Nebr.
(Envelope: B 38 P. a. m. Monsieur ——— ——— —— ——— ——— street N. Y. City.)

a The girl who wrote this letter was formerly in a disorderly house in New York City and went to the West after the places were closed in New York.

106

My stable has enlarged a bit. I entered a 2-year-old in the race three weeks ago. I sent her to Redding, Cal., so I expect to go there about April 1, leaving Lizzie here alone, as business is kind of bum here at present and I have over $10 a day expenses. I will give Lizzie a chance to save her money here.

The following is a copy of a letter taken in a raid:

DAWSON, YUKON TERRITORY, CANADA,
February 21, 1908.

DEAR FRIEND: How are you and how is your business getting along? I am ready to fill my pockets as soon as business picks up in Dawson. The winter has not been very cold at all. I am going to Seattle for the exposition, and I will go to France in 1911 for the exposition of Paris. The dance halls are closed here. I went back to Klondike City and I will get on very well. It is quite a time since I received any news from you. I received a letter from Louis from Theims; he will be in New York in the month of September. I see nothing more to say, except I embrace you with all my heart.
　　　Your friend,
　　　　　　　　　　　　　　　　　　　MATILD.

Tell me, have they come to get the trunks I left with you?

Another letter, showing the interstate character of the traffic, was found at the French Club in New York City, a copy of which is set out below:

FRIEND ARTHUR: I received your letter and I hurry to answer. It was a long time since I heard from you. My poor friend business is more than bad. We have the famous fleet in the bay. Business is worse than ever, due to a crowd. Everywhere great confusion. The policemen have the right to reprimand anybody, and if they do so, they are made game of.

These sailors go in bands; most of them have not been paid here; also they leave on Friday, 15. What luck! You talk about me. I have put my woman to work and sold my house in Oakland, $2,000—$1,000 cash and the other $1,000 July 1—but that I am afraid I shall lose. That does not work with me. If they do not pay, I shall take back the house to give it to anybody I please. I shall lose $750, but shall be happy to be relieved of it. At Frisco there are more houses than women, and new houses open every day. For that reason there are not a few houses for sale. They have no women, and the running expenses bring wretchedness to this entire section. From everywhere I hear business is very bad, and in many houses they are sending away men and women. I wonder what I can do.

I hear ——— ——— has sold his house at Chicago at a good price. What a country of villians! In rivalry they eat the flesh skin off one another alive. There is an establishment here, the best of all, only $20,000; it is worth it, certainly. The keepers no longer agree.

It is splendid, and the finest house. It is new, the first to be opened after the fire; 28 rooms, each one more beautiful than the other. It is the only one that has permanent inmates. Oh! but they are doing a good business.

If you want further information, I am ready to give it to you.

I hear Auguste has no more ——— and he is better, but I have not seen him for a long time, for it is not agreeable to go through that establishment with that band of ——— which is always there.

I am going to write to Maurice to-morrow. As far as the cribs are concerned here, I think it is all up with them, unfortunately. I have written to Portland to one of my friends, and if I have good news I will go there to see the layout of the land. I am tired of it here.

Best regards to your woman from Marthe, also from me.
　　　Expecting to hear from you soon,
　　　　　　　　　　　　　　　　　　　CAMILE.

For your friend who was just arrested I am very sorry. Well, this will cost him a lot of money. It is very dangerous, this kind of business. A person has to be mighty careful. I have seen it coming. Here in Chicago the trouble is not over yet. (Letter p. —.)

Another:
* * * I have it from reliable sources that the immigration government and the government officers and the secret service are after me, * * *. (Letter, p. —.)

Appendix VII–A.

LETTERS AND AFFIDAVIT.

SEATTLE, WASH., *October 22, 1908.*

Mrs. ——— ———, *New York City.*

DEAR MADAM: I suppose you have received letter from Mr. G. about the whole affair, as I told whole thing to him and asked him to write the matter to you.

Now, the lady from Spokane and Mr. ——— done their best to secure the cigars and they got ready with 4 cigars which we can send to you most any time, but each of them want $300 to pay their debts before they leave here, and Mrs. ———, of Spokane, will be responsible for all of them which will be sent this time; and I think it is entirely safe proposition to you, as Mrs. ——— owns big hotel and laundry in Spokane City, and she is considered to be trustworthy lady among the society.

Will you kindly wire me as soon as you receive this letter, as Mrs. ——— is staying in the city for that purpose alone and her business affairs in Spokane compel her to return to Spokane as soon as possible.

Wishing this proposition will be satisfactory to you and hoping to hear from you soon, I remain,

Yours, truly,   ——— ———.

SEATTLE, WASH., *October 22, 1908.*

MY DEAR MRS. ———: I have just been to see the cigars; they are fine, young, and good looking; he has four of them, but it seems that they are in debt here to the extent of $300 each; that is for their fare and other expenses for bringing them from Japan, and the party here wants that money. Now, if you feel like advancing them $300 each, they are ready to go at once, and ——— will go with them. This money you will get back as the cigars earn it. Mrs. ——— will take all responsibility of these cigars staying with you until all debts are paid, and told me that she would sign an agreement to that effect, and I have found out that she is a responsible person; you know her; she owns a house in Spokane. Now, if this suits you, wire the money at once. Don't delay. Together with 5 fares; that is, transportation for 5, ——— —you can settle with him when he gets there. You can send me $100 for my expenses and pay. I have been put out quite a little; I had to lay my boat up two days in order to make this trip; but I told you I would see you through this thing, and of course I will do as I promised. I think that when ——— gets back, and reports favorable that you will have no trouble in getting all you need; and if you work it right, you will have a monopoly on the Japanese goods in New York City, because you are dealing with the right people at this end of the line. If you send the money to me, wire it to my address at Bellingham. I had ought to hear from you in six days from date. I hope that you will understand this fully. The cigars must have $300 each (advance), ($1,200), together with 5 fares, whatever that is. You can find out there how much that will be, and whenever that comes I will see to it that they will start east on the next train and will wire you accordingly, so that you will know when to look for them. I have also taken the matter up fully with ———, in order to guard against any crooked work, and he has pledged himself to me that everything will be done on the square.

Hoping that everything will be satisfactory with you, I beg to remain yours, with my very best wishes.

——— ———.

AFFIDAVIT.

STATE OF NEW YORK,
County of New York, ss:

——— ———, being duly sworn, deposes and says that he is acquainted with many of the inmates of the restricted districts in Seattle; that he is acquainted with the keepers of the houses of prostitution in Seattle, with many of the pimps, and has a knowledge of the system under which they all work; that in his opinion the word "slavery" is none too strong a word to use in explaining the conditions which surround many of the immigrant girls in Seattle who are in the United States in violation of section 3 of the immigration act; that most of the said immigrant girls are in debt to their procurer or the disorderly house keeper to such an extent that she has no possible chance of paying it off; in fact, as soon as one debt is paid by her another is imposed upon her. It is part of the system of the business to keep the inmates of the disorderly houses so hopelessly in debt that they give up all hope of gaining their freedom. This is done by a system of charges made against them for their board, their house clothes, and their transportation from place to place in the United States, and the expense of first importation into the country. Deponent knows one Japanese prostitute in Seattle who was imported into the United States for immoral purposes when a young girl. She is now 40 years of age, and has never had an income except that derived from practicing prostitution. She told deponent that it took her sixteen years constant work to get herself out of debt and gain her freedom. She said she had been saving her earnings for four years last past and had saved over $2,000. _____ _____.

Sworn to before me this 6th day of November, 1909. _____ _____.

O

SELECT BIBLIOGRAPHY

Barnard, William F. *Forty Years at the Five Points. A Sketch of the Five Points House of Industry.* New York: Five Points House of Industry, 1893.

Barrell, Charles Wisner. "The Real Drama of the Slums, as told in John Sloan's Etchings." *The Craftsman.* 15 (1909): 559-64.

Bell, Ernest A. *Fighting the Traffic in Young Girls, or War on the White Slave Trade.* New York: Nichols, 1910.

Bennett, Helen Christine. *American Women in Civic Work.* New York: Dodd, Mead, 1915.

Betts, Lillian W. *The Leaven in a Great City.* New York: Dodd, Mead, 1903.

Bliss, William D. P., ed. *The Encyclopedia of Social Reforms.* New York: Funk and Wagnalls, 1898.

Bliss, William D. P., ed. *The New Encyclopedia of Social Reforms.* New York: Funk and Wagnalls, 1910.

Booth, William. *In Darkest England and the Way Out.* (London: International Headquarters of the Salvation Army, 1890; Reprinted with a Foreword by Francesco Cordasco, New York: Garrett Press, 1970).

Brace, Charles Loring. *The Dangerous Classes of New York and Twenty Years Work Among Them.* New York: Wynkoop and Hallenbeck, 1872.

Bremner, Robert H., *et al.,* eds. *Childhood and Youth in America: A Documentary History.* 3 vols. in 5 vols. Cambridge: Harvard University Press, 1971-1974.

Bruère, Robert W. "The Conquest of Poverty. A Socialist Solution of the Problem." *Metropolitan Magazine.* 33 (1909-10): 651-60.

Bruère, Robert W. "The Good Samaritan, Incorporated." *Harper's Monthly Magazine.* 120 (1909-10): 833-38.

Bruno, Frank J. *Trends in Social Work as Reflected in the Proceedings of the National Conference of Social Work, 1874-1946.* New York: Columbia University Press, 1948.

Buel, J. W. *Metropolitan Life Unveiled; or the Mysteries and Miseries of America's Great Cities.* St. Louis: Historical Publishing Company, 1882.

Butler, Elizabeth B. *Women and the Trades.* New York: Charities Publication, 1910.

Campbell, Helen. "Certain Convictions as to Poverty." *The Arena.* 1 (1889-90): 101-13.

Campbell, Helen. *Prisoners of Poverty. Women Wage-Earners, Their Trades and Their Lives.* Boston: Roberts Brothers, 1887.

Campbell, Helen. "White Child Slavery." *The Arena.* 1 (1889-90): 589-91.

Campbell, Helen. *Women Wage-Earners. Their Past, Their Present, and Their Future.* Boston: Roberts Brothers, 1893.

Campbell, Helen. "The Working Women of Today." *The Arena.* 4 (1891): 329-39.

Campbell, Helen, et al. *Darkness and Daylight: or Lights and Shadows of New York Life. A Woman's Narrative.* Hartford: A. D. Worthington and Company, 1891.

Chapin, Robert Coit. *The Standard of Living Among Workingmen's Families in New York City.* New York: Charities Publication Committee, 1909.

Community Service Society of New York. *Frontiers in Human Welfare. The Story of a Hundred Years of Service to the Community of New York, 1848-1948.* New York: Community Service Society of New York, 1948.

Connelly, Mark T. *The Response to Prostitution in the Progressive Era.* Chapel Hill: University of North Carolina Press, 1980.

Cordasco, Francesco. *Italian Immigrants Abroad: A Bibliography on the Italian Experience Outside Italy in Europe, the Americas, Australia, and Africa/ Emigrazione E Lavoro Italiano All'Estero: Repertorio Bibliografico.* Detroit: Blaine Ethridge-Books, 1979. (Originally published Rome: Ministero Degli Affari Esteri, 1967.)

Cordasco, Francesco. *Jacob Riis Revisited: Poverty and the Slum in Another Era.* New York: Doubleday, 1968.

Cordasco, Francesco. "Charles Loring Brace and the Dangerous Classes: Historical Analogues of the Urban Black Poor." *Journal of Human Relations.* 20 (3rd Quarter 1972): 379-386.

Cordasco, Francesco. "Street Arabs and Gutter Snipes." *Journal of Human Relations.* 20 (3rd Quarter 1972): 387-390.

Crane, Stephen. *Maggie, a Girl of the Streets.* New York: Newland Press, 1893.

Davis, Allen F. *Spearheads for Reform: The Social Settlements and the Progressive Movement, 1890-1914.* New York: Oxford University Press, 1967.

Davis, Allen F. *American Heroine: The Life and Legend of Jane Addams.* New York: Oxford University Press, 1973.

Feldman, Egal. "Prostitution, the Alien Woman and the Progressive Imagination, 1910-1915." *American Quarterly.* 19 (Summer 1967): 192-206.

Flower, B. O. *Civilization's Inferno; or, Studies in the Social Cellar.* Boston: Arena Publishing Company, 1893.

Hamilton, Alice. *Exploring the Dangerous Trades. The Autobiography of Alice Hamilton, M.D.* Boston: Little, Brown, 1943.

Hunter, Robert. "A Plea for the Investigation of the Conditions Affecting the Length of Trade Life." *The Annals.* 27 (1906): 500-503.

Hunter, Robert. *Poverty.* New York: The Macmillan Company, 1904.

Hunter, Robert. "The Relation between Social Settlements and Charity Organization." *Journal of Political Economy.* 11 (1902-3): 75-88.

Kauffman, Reginald W. *The House of Bondage.* New York: Grosset & Dunlap, 1910.

Kellor, Frances A. *Out of Work. A Study of Employment Agencies: Their Treatment of the Unemployed, and Their Influence upon Homes and Business.* New York: G. P. Putnam's Sons, 1905.

Kellor, Frances A. *Out of Work. A Study of Unemployment.* New York: G. P. Putnam's Sons, 1915.

Kneeland, George J. *Commercialized Prostitution in New York City.* New York: The Century Company, 1913.

Lowell, Josephine Shaw. "Methods of Relief for the Unemployed." *The Forum.* 16 (1893-94): 655-62.

Lowell, Josephine Shaw. *Public Relief and Private Charity.* New York: G.P. Putnam's Sons, 1884.

Lowell, Josephine Shaw. "The True Aim of Charity Organization Societies." *The Forum.* 21 (1896): 494-500.

Mindel, Charles H. and Robert W. Habenstein, eds. *Ethnic Families in America.* New York: Elsevier, 1976.

New York Association for Improving the Condition of the Poor. *Fighting Poverty. What the A.I.C.P. Does to Eliminate the Causes of Distress and to Prevent Their Recurrence.* New York: New York A.I.C.P., 1912.

Ralph, Julian. *People We Pass. Stories of Life Among the Masses of New York City.* New York: Harper and Brothers, 1896.

Readers Guide to Periodical Literature. (Under the subject heading "Prostitution," the *RGPL* lists 36 entries for the period 1890-1909; 156 entries for the period 1910-1914; and 41 entries for the period 1915-1924).

Richardson, Dorothy. "The Difficulties and Dangers Confronting the Working Woman." *The Annals.* 27 (1906): 624-26.

Richardson, Dorothy. *The Long Day. The Story of a New York Working Girl as Told by Herself.* New York: The Century Company, 1906.

Richmond, Mary Ellen. *Friendly Visiting Among the Poor. A Handbook for Charity Workers.* New York: The Macmillan Company, 1899.

Riis, Jacob A. *The Children of the Poor.* New York: Charles Scribner's Sons, 1892. Reprinted with an introduction by Francesco Cordasco, New York: Garrett Press, 1970.

Riis, Jacob A. "The Children of the Poor." *Scribner's Magazine.* 11 (1892): 531-56.

Riis, Jacob A. *How the Other Half Lives.* New York: Charles Scribner's Sons, 1890. Reprinted with an introduction by Francesco Cordasco, New York: Garrett Press, 1970.

Riis, Jacob A. *The Making of an American.* New York: The Macmillan Company, 1903.

Riis, Jacob A. "Special Needs of the Poor in New York." *The Forum.* 14 (1892-93): 492-502.

Riis, Jacob A. "The Tenement House Exhibition." *Harper's Weekly.* 64 (1900): 104.

Riis, Jacob A. *A Ten Years' War. An Account of the Battle with the Slum in New York.* Boston: Houghton Mifflin, 1900.

Simkhovitch, Mary Kingsbury. *Neighborhood, My Story of Greenwich House.* New York: W. W. Norton, 1938.

Simkhovitch, Mary Kingsbury and Elizabeth Ogg. *Quicksand, the Way of Life in the Slums.* Evanston, Illinois: Row, Peterson, 1946.

"Tenement Life in New York." *Harper's Weekly.* 23 (1879): 246 and 266-67.

Townsend, Edward W. *A Daughter of the Tenements.* New York: Lovell, Coryell, 1895.

True, Ruth S. *The Neglected Girl.* New York: Survey Associates, 1914.

Turner, George K. "The Daughters of the Poor." *McClure's Magazine.* 34 (1909-1910): 45-61.

United States. Bureau of Labor. *Report on Conditions of Woman and Child Wage Earners in the United States.* 19 vols. Washington: Government Printing Office, 1910-1913.

United States. Commissioner of Labor. *Seventh Special Report . . . The Slums of Baltimore, Chicago, New York and Philadelphia.* Washington: Government Printing Office, 1894. Reprinted with A New Foreword by Francesco Cordasco, New York: Garrett Press, 1970.

Van Kleeck, Mary. *Artificial Flower Makers.* New York: Russell Sage Foundation, 1913.

Van Kleeck, Mary. *A Seasonal Industry. A Study of the Millinery Trade in New York.* New York: Russell Sage Foundation, 1917.

Van Kleeck, Mary. *Women in the Bookbinding Trade.* New York: Russell Sage Foundation, 1913.

Van Kleeck, Mary. "The Workers' Bill for Unemployment." *The New Republic.* 81 (1934-35): 121-24.

Van Kleeck, Mary. "Working Hours of Women in Factories." *Charities and the Commons.* 17 (1906): 13-21.

Van Vorst, Mrs. John, and Marie Van Vorst. *The Woman Who Toils, Being the Experiences of Two Gentlewomen as Factory Girls.* New York: Doubleday, Page, 1903.

Wald, Lillian D. *The House on Henry Street.* New York: Henry Holt, 1915.

Walkowitz, Judity, R. *Prostitution and Victorian Society: Women, Class and the State.* Cambridge: Cambridge University Press, 1980.

Watson, Frank Dekker. *The Charity Organization Movement in the United States. A Study in American Philanthropy.* New York: The Macmillan Company, 1922.

Weller, Charles Frederick. *Neglected Neighbors. Stories of Life in the Alleys, Tenements and Shanties of the National Capital.* Philadelphia: John C. Winston, 1908.

Woods, Robert A. *Americans in Process.* Boston: Houghton Mifflin, 1902.

Woods, Robert A., ed. *The City Wilderness.* Boston and New York: Houghton Mifflin, 1899. Reprinted with a new introduction by David N. Alloway, New York: Garrett Press, 1970.

Woods, Robert A., *et al. The Poor in Great Cities.* New York: Charles Scribner's Sons, 1895.

Woolf, Michael Angelo. *Sketches of Lowly Life in a Great City.* New York: G. P. Putnam's Sons, 1899.

INDEX